PRAISE FO

APP

"When one of the companies I worked for needed help taking its consulting organization to the next level, I hired Steve Shu. His ability to drive our management team - all with different opinions on what we should or should not do - to a 'so-what' conclusion and pragmatic next steps gave us the jump start we needed. He is one of the best and deeply understands how consulting organizations should work. His book provides great techniques as well as tools you can use immediately."

- Prakash Panjwani, CEO at WatchGuard Technologies, former President and CEO of SafeNet

"Steve Shu has put together a comprehensive guide to the all-important nuts and bolts of being a great consultant. The information in Chapter 21, 'Eight Secret Weapons of the Modern Consultant,' is worth the price of the book. If you're serious about being a more effective consultant, read this book."

- Michael McLaughlin, Author of Winning the Professional Services Sale and Principal Consultant at MindShare Consulting LLC

"I've worked with Steve Shu on consulting projects related to innovation and the application of behavioral science principles. He is very well respected by both academics and professionals. And as a professor in the management and organizations area, and someone who has a son working as a management consultant, it's great to see a book like his that addresses nuances of the profession of consulting."

- John W. Payne, Joseph J. Ruvane Professor of Business Administration at the Fuqua School of Business, Duke University

"Steve provides a thorough guide full of practical recommendations on how to drive any initiative to a positive outcome. If you are in a business to serve customers (internal and external), this is an essential read for you whether you're in a Fortune-50 company or a startup, or a management consultant. I found at least eight compelling and insightful recommendations that I can apply today in my technology startup to improve my relationship with my customers and partners."

- Anurag Khaitan, Venture Investor, Entrepreneur; former General Manager of Sprint Nextel Ventures and management consultant with PRTM

"Steve Shu has written a hands-on, highly practical guide for new management consultants and internal corporate business strategists alike. So many projects fail because they do not practice the basic consulting project management hygiene Steve describes in chapter 11. If you are new to the trade and want to greatly increase your chance of delivering successful consulting projects, read this book."

- Robert Reppa, Vice President Strategy at Johnson Controls and former Partner at Booz & Company

"Steve Shu has written a Rosetta Stone for both new and experienced consultants. Filled with forty power-packed ideas and practical chapter takeaways, Consulting Apprenticeship is structured for busy executives to easily digest each concept. A must read for those who seek to go beyond the shallow bromides of the consulting profession, and hone their skills with deeper, more meaningful approaches."

- Adrian C. Ott, Award-winning author of *The 24-Hour Customer*, and CEO, Exponential Edge Inc, called "One of Silicon Valley's most respected strategists" by Consulting Magazine

The Consulting Apprenticeship

Steve Shu

Published by Steve Shu Consulting Services

steveshuconsulting.com

DEDICATION

Dedicated to my wife, my kids, my brother, and my parents who each gave significant decades of their lives to enrich my own.

CONTENTS

THE CONSULTING APPRENTICESHIP

I started blogging on September 2, 2004 as an experiment, a sandbox of sorts to play in. I had no idea what to expect since blogs were only just starting to cross the chasm and go mainstream. In 2004, Merriam-Webster added the term "blog" to the dictionary (Merriam-Webster, Incorporated n.d.). By the end of 2006, Time Magazine had an iconic cover with "You" as Person of the Year (Time, Inc. 2006), a significant historical marker for the volume of end-user generated content, whether on YouTube, MySpace, or any number of other social media and network platforms. Blogging succeeded as a new medium because it went beyond traditional publishing – people could both bypass big media and converse person to person through threaded streams of comments on blog posts. People could reach others around the world, and they mostly used blogs to share their personal lives and participate in political debates. Publish once. Converse everywhere.

During those early years of the rise of the blog, there was relatively little serious business content on blogs. And while it took me awhile to find my own voice in this new media space, I was suddenly conversing with people around the world about business topics. I started exchanging blog comments and emails with professionals and consultants from all around the United States, Canada, the United Kingdom, Germany, India, Singapore, Japan, Australia, South America, and Africa. People were interested in what I had to say on management, and especially, about the management consulting industry, a largely mysterious and misunderstood profession.

A subset of material that generated significant interest was regarding my perspectives on consulting thinking and techniques. I wrote – sometimes out of necessity to train others on the practice of consulting - about ideas that were not written about elsewhere. My purpose was to fill a gap in the transfer of knowledge and exchange of ideas. Many management and consulting ideas are taught based on an apprenticeship model. Hence, few write down such ideas for general consumption. Senior consultants pass on tacit knowledge on to more junior consultants. Peer executives share this type of knowledge with other executives. Some managers learn on the job. I developed this book largely because I enjoy teaching and wanted to leave my mark on the field. To create the book content, I revisited past blog posts that have stood the test of time, refreshed certain ideas, and added new material.

I didn't want to reinvent the world and write a comprehensive book on consulting or even a comprehensive book on a sliver of the field. For example, there are a number of books that I often recommend for the core ideas around consulting. These include *The McKinsey Way* for a general overview of consulting (Rasiel 1999), *Process Consultation* for details on influencing work situations without formal authority (Schein 1988), *Flawless Consulting* especially for those coming from engineering or non-consulting backgrounds (Block 2011), and *The Pyramid Principle* for honing skills around writing and structuring thoughts in a business context (Minto 2010). There are also a number of good books on consulting sales and marketing, firm management, and evolution of the industry.

The Consulting Apprenticeship is written for business professionals and consultants with a focus on nuances passed on during apprenticeship regarding consulting delivery (i.e., the execution of consulting-style projects). *The Consulting Apprenticeship* can be read standalone or as a complement to the aforementioned books. Business professionals can benefit with a jump-start approach to applying consulting principles to their business. New consultants may learn some things that their mentors haven't covered. Mid- to senior-level consultants may benefit through reinforcement and reflecting on mastery of the consulting approach.

Designed for the busy professional, *The Consulting Apprenticeship* is a book of forty, quick-read ideas. Think of these ideas as three-minute coaching, or idea sharing sessions that you might get from a mentor or peer. These forty, short chapters are divided into four sections:

- **Consulting Mindset** – This section covers consulting ways of thinking and can be adopted by both company personnel and consultants.
- **Consulting Techniques** – This section covers specific tactics and toolkit methods when using consultative approaches in the trenches as either a company- or consulting firm-practitioner.
- **Consulting Mastery** – This section covers advanced perspectives on consulting and may be more useful to either company personnel evaluating consultants or mid- to senior-level consultants.
- **Consulting Special Situations** – Whereas the prior sections are applicable to a wide variety of situations, this section covers more infrequent, specific business situations involving consultative approaches in the trenches as either a company- or consulting firm-practitioner.

Each chapter of the book concludes with an optional, takeaway exercise. The exercises vary widely in terms of level of involvement. For example, in some cases you can simply refer to online material I provide or reference. In other cases, you can engage in deeper thinking or apply the concepts over an extended period of time.

However you choose to use this book, consulting mastery is a lifelong pursuit. I hope this book helps you with your journey.

Stephen Shu

SECTION ONE: CONSULTING MINDSET

1
THE POWER OF PROJECT-BASED THINKING

Projects[1] are the core of consulting. Whereas operating companies may or may not have projects, practically everything in a consulting business is connected to a project. Among key benefits, projects connect specific desired outcomes with business activities. Example projects could include: determining the overall business strategy for a multi-business unit company, incubating a new business unit, relaunching a professional services business, developing a new mobile software application, rebranding a product line, or optimizing manufacturing processes for regional business expansion.

Yet too often I have seen organizations go on autopilot and simply engage in performing activities without clarity about the bigger picture. Statements are made, such as "We need to set up a meeting with our software vendor," or "We should research the pricing policies of our top competitor," or "We need to develop content to support our distribution partner." Performing activities without purpose often leads to inefficiencies.[2] What is the big picture? Are there end goals?

[1] Projects are often referred to as engagements, especially in the case of 3rd-party consulting projects.

[2] Even more vivid is the quote often attributed to the famous

Are these goals part of a well-defined project?

Introducing project-based thinking can help many company efforts. Here are some benefits I have seen from incorporating project-based thinking:

- Since project life can end at any moment, fewer things are taken for granted.
- Projects can improve the communication patterns within an organization.
- Projects can increase focus on outputs and measureable results.
- A focus on outputs can lead to quicker decisions.
- Excess capacity and process inefficiencies become more readily exposed.
- A need for quicker decisions increases the need for management to articulate strategic tradeoffs more crisply.
- The concrete nature of projects makes it easier for management to balance benefits (e.g., revenue) against costs (e.g., expenses) and investment levels.
- The concentrated goal of executing a project can help an organization break through barriers and corporate inertia.
- A focus on project goals can bring out the best leadership qualities of a team.

Takeaway Exercise: Assess how your organization or client engages in activities. How do current activities contribute to a larger goal? To what extent can goals be articulated? How might a project-based approach for organizing activities around clear goals and milestones help get things on track or improve performance?

---

strategist and Chinese military general, Sun Tzu: "Tactics without strategy is the noise before defeat." The quote attribution is probably apocryphal with the actual author unknown.

2
ENGAGEMENT MANAGEMENT IS THE ESSENCE OF MANAGEMENT CONSULTING

Between different consulting firms and practices, the job responsibilities and experience levels of engagement managers vary widely. There is one characteristic of the position that captures the essence of management consulting better than characteristics of other typical consulting positions (e.g., principal, partner, director, associate, manager). By understanding the central function of engagement management, one can better understand the essence of management consulting.

Engagement managers own the problem statement from the perspective of the customer, and thus have the responsibility to ensure that project team both structures and executes the problem-solving methodology correctly.

Consider an example where a client needs help to figure out whether they should enter a wireless business, identify under what circumstances it makes sense, define the strategy and plan for how it should be done, and get cross-functional buy-in from the management team and Board of Directors. In this case, the engagement manager may need to work with the project team to synthesize primary and secondary marketing research from end users and distributors, construct financial analyses, develop technology scenarios and architectures, conduct client workshops on various subjects to gain insights and share best practice perspectives, perform gap analyses between present methods of operations and desired future states, or perform competitive analyses and forecasting.

Another problem statement might be "Figure out the root cause of declining customer satisfaction and fix it because my internal management team is giving me mixed messages." Yet another one might be "How do I transform my business from doing lots of low margin X to doing more high margin Y."

In essence, the role of the engagement manager is to help the client solve their problems by synthesizing the work of smart people and subject matter experts in different functions and areas from throughout the consulting firm and client organization. As a quick digression, one should note that setting up the problem statement properly is very key to selling consulting engagements and solving them – do not take it for granted that the problem statement is articulated properly.

In closing, I find that people frequently confuse the role of project managers with that of engagement managers. There are definitely some overlapping functions, but the essence of project management is more to ensure that things are accomplished on time, on budget, and according to customer specifications. On the other hand, the role of the engagement manager is to own the client problem statement as if it were their own. At risk of sounding like I am diminishing the importance of the function, project management becomes more of an execution detail in the greater scheme of things.

Takeaway Exercise: Assess to what extent your organization has engagement managers leading projects. Do the engagement managers keep a close eye on the problem statements for their projects? If you are a practitioner within a company or consulting firm, observe an engagement (perhaps run by another engagement manager) that utilizes a new approach to addressing a problem statement.

3
ARTICULATING AND REARTICULATING PROBLEM STATEMENTS

Engineering and management consulting share a common feature - each discipline tends to be very problem-solving oriented. In engineering, one may be posed the problem of trying to figure out the optimal circuit or filter for minimizing noise from a radio station transmission. There are structured, mathematical ways for solving such problems. On the other hand, management consultants may be posed the problem of figuring out the market opportunity and business strategy for a company to extend its product line for a subset of the total customer base. There are common business methodologies for addressing these types of problems too.

To pick on consulting, sometimes it's very tempting to disappear and run off and solve the problem that's been articulated in the statement of work signed with the client. But, I think that it's also important to have a good client relationship and regular communication structure that enable the problem statement to be adjusted and refined. As an example, for some of the engagements I have overseen, I asked consulting teams to write down the problem statement in their own words near the beginning of the project (which may sometimes be a list of key questions in paragraph form that the customer has asked plus the objectives of the project) while refining the problem statement to a finer level of detail throughout the project. At the end of the project, the consultant can put the refined problem statement at beginning of the final executive presentation. Highlighting the problem statement reaffirms the need for the project and consultant.

So while at the beginning of an engagement, a problem statement might be something like "Purpose of project will be to determine the technology strategy for widgets," in the end the refined problem statement might be "Purpose of the project is to address the following: 1) Determine the business attractiveness of A, B, and C services in the widget market. 2) Identify technology options for approaching the market and tradeoffs. 3) Perform full financial assessment of options, including worst-case walkaway price for an upcoming auction, which is prerequisite for one of the service areas. 4) Determine optimal business model for approaching market, which includes consideration of leasing versus buy and own models."

By both breaking the problem statement down to a lower level of granularity and repositioning the statement for accuracy, it becomes easier to determine whether the team is solving the right problem. Dividing the problem in such a way allows different consultants attack the pieces.

Although I'm not much into social commentary, consider what has been going on with Iran since 2007 with nuclear fuel and the interests of both Iran and the United States. From the perspective of the US it seems as though some have articulated the problem statement as being, "How do we prevent weapons-grade nuclear fuel from getting into the wrong hands?" Just for argument's purposes, what if the problem statement was rearticulated to be, "How do we help countries to achieve their nuclear energy goals while preventing weapons-grade nuclear fuel from getting into the wrong hands?" With a refined problem statement, one might think of more tailored approaches for addressing each issue, such as supporting or even funding nuclear energy goals, while requiring monitoring for process control purposes.

Or consider an easier problem. Suppose a significant other poses you the problem of finding the best nonstop flight between Los Angeles and New York City. What if the problem statement was rearticulated to finding the cheapest airfare between the two cities? Such a problem statement might open up possibilities to less expensive flights by allowing for intermediate stops in other cities. Or what if the problem statement was to find the most relaxing way to travel between the two cities? This problem statement might yield solutions that provide for a lot of time to sleep in, pampering through upgraded seats, and chauffeured transport to and from the airport.

The real point is that rearticulating problem statements can often lead to better outcomes, stimulate creative ideas, and offer opportunities for teams to get around roadblocks.

Takeaway Exercise 1: **Take a moment to write down the problem statement for a project you or your company is working on. How general or specific is the current problem statement? How might the problem statement be refined?**

Takeaway Exercise 2: **If you want to spend more time on core problem solving in consulting, it is worthwhile to better understand how to establish the right structure. The purpose of The Consulting Apprenticeship is not to re-invent the wheel. I encourage you to consider some other resources I've listed at http://steveshuconsulting.com/2010/01/chap3-consulting-apprenticeship. Bread and butter consulting concepts like issue trees, "mutually exclusive, collectively exhaustive" (MECE), and the 80/20 rule are covered there.**

4
AN EXAMPLE OF CONSULTING ENGAGEMENT WORKSTREAMS

The term "workstream" is often used in consulting, but I have not seen where it is defined for new consultants to reference. A workstream is an important concept that often ties to consulting proposals, engagement management, division of labor, and processes used with the client. Not every consulting firm characterizes workstreams the way I do, but I have found similar structures used by many consulting organizations.

What is a workstream and where does it fit in the context of a consulting engagement? Let's start with the latter question first.

A consulting engagement is set of consulting activities designed to solve a specific problem statement for a client. In the prior chapter, I hinted that a consulting problem statement usually must be decomposed into smaller problems statements. The problem statement can be thought of as a tree of problem statements with the master problem statement being comprised of sub-problem statements.

The figure below depicts the engagement structure for a project I managed. The master problem statement was "to help the client develop a business strategy and plan for entering the market as a new entrant in the wireless network and applications provider space." Sub-problem statements included:

- **Strategy questions** - How should the company look at services that it both currently offers and wants to offer? How competitive are the markets? What business models can be used to offer services?
- **Technology questions** - What technology options does the company have based on the options to approach the business? What is the magnitude of the technology effort that would need to be involved?
- **Finance questions** - What do the financials look like for the various business models? Can calibrate these models against other companies?
- **Communication and steering questions** - What is the best way to get the right people in the organization involved, financing approved, and efforts mobilized if the plan makes sense?

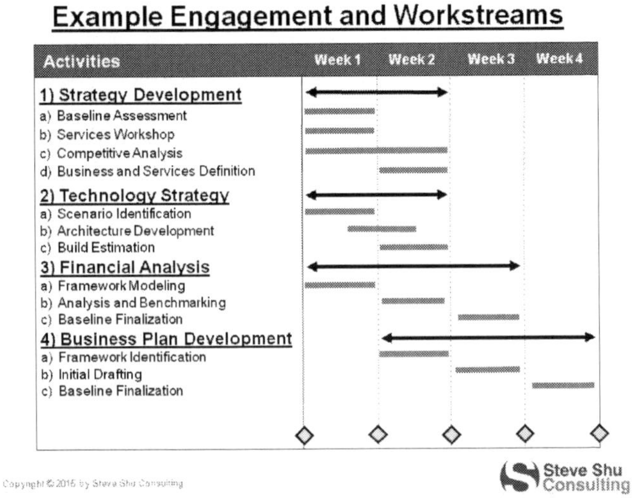

Example Engagement and Workstreams

Activities | Week 1 | Week 2 | Week 3 | Week 4

1) Strategy Development
a) Baseline Assessment
b) Services Workshop
c) Competitive Analysis
d) Business and Services Definition
2) Technology Strategy
a) Scenario Identification
b) Architecture Development
c) Build Estimation
3) Financial Analysis
a) Framework Modeling
b) Analysis and Benchmarking
c) Baseline Finalization
4) Business Plan Development
a) Framework Identification
b) Initial Drafting
c) Baseline Finalization

Steve Shu Consulting

Downloadable figure available at: http://steveshuconsulting.com/2000/01/download-figures-the-consulting-apprenticeship

So to address the master problem and sub-problem

statements, engagement activities are organized into coarse groupings called workstreams. The prior figure has four workstreams covering strategy, technology, finance, and business plan development. For example, the top workstream covers strategy development. Activities within the workstream include assessing the current business services, conducting a workshop to brainstorm services, performing a competitive assessment of the company and its environment, and defining the business model and services to be offered. The bottom workstream includes collaborative efforts to combine findings and recommendations for the project into a cohesive package for presentation to the company's board. Note that each workstream has a prime consultant and prime client point of contact assigned. The overall engagement structure is similar to standard project management practices; additional key considerations from a consulting perspective are alignment with the problem statement and consultant-client touch points.

To close off this discussion, it is important to establish a cadence and regular review structure with the client. I'll touch on this a bit more in the Chapter 11: In Consulting the Process is an Essential Part of the Deliverable.

Takeaway Exercise: Develop an engagement structure by writing down the problem statement for a project and setting up a timeline of workstream activities to address the problem statement. Use a top-down structure so that the problem statement, a summary timeline like the one above, and a description of the activities might collectively be included in a written proposal to management to perform the work.

5
CLIENT FACILITATION SKILLS

When I first started as a management consultant back at Pittiglio Rabin Todd & McGrath (acquired by PwC) (PwC Completes Acquisition of PRTM 2011), one of the hardest things for me to grasp was the concept of "client facilitation." Many of the consultants I knew were eager to apply standard frameworks in business schools like Five Forces (for competitive and profitability analysis), net present value (NPV), financial analysis tools, statistical regression, and the marketing 3Cs/STP/4Ps, but few talked about client facilitation in explicit terms.

In my mind, client facilitation refers to the processes and skills that a consultant uses to get a client organization to critical decision points, deep understanding, and commitment to move forward or redirect.

A master of client facilitation is a person that can:

- **Master analysis skills of the trade** – Consultants need to be able to use top-down logical reasoning, use many analytical frameworks, and work analyses from multiple directions.
- **Communicate well** – Consultants need be proficient with many communication mediums, whether via face-to-face conversations, written documents, phone, text messaging, etc.

- **Teach and frame things properly** - Because interactions with parties vary widely and parties often have varying levels of knowledge, consultants must be able to ramp-up conversations quickly and put them in the proper context.
- **Recognize the state of an organization's progress and how decisions are made** – Consultants need to develop street smarts. Is the marketing department behind in their understanding? Who does the CEO look to as his/her right hand? If needed, what steps are needed to get the right hand person on board and up-to-speed? How can the consulting team get things to move forward past a roadblock? Can it be done in one step or will it take two steps?
- **Lead people without formal authority** – As a consultant, can you educate people, empathize with the organization, get the organization to trust you, pave a vision, and outline a set of tradeoffs with such clarity that motion must happen?

In my opinion, the last skill is the most important. The essence of client facilitation is leading people effectively without formally being in charge.

Takeaway Exercise: Rate yourself on scale of 1 to 10 in the areas of analysis, communication, teaching and framing, street smarts, and leading without authority. Set a concrete action plan for improving one of these areas over the next three to six months.

6
HUNTING VERSUS FISHING LICENSES

Very often consulting engagements will include diagnostics or assessments early on in the process. An assessment may help a client quickly zero in on where major problems are and focus business improvement efforts. For example, an operations improvement project may span many business units and the work of thousands of people. An operational assessment may contain numerous data collection and interview activities to help determine what aspect of organizational resources, process, and systems could be improved. Assessment activities are a critical part of the engagement. With these engagements, if one gets garbage in, one gets garbage out.

In comes the motivation for obtaining a "hunting license." As one can imagine, consultants may need to get very sensitive information in order to help a client analyze what is going on. When working in the trenches, individuals within the client's organization may be reluctant to give the consultant information. If a consultant has been given an adequate hunting license, essentially an authorization by a manager or executive to obtain operational data needed, a consultant can better navigate through the client organization and obtain information needed.

Consultants need to recognize that their hunting licenses do not generally mean that they have a right to "fish for information." When consultants seek information and interview workers in the trenches, they should have a clear goal in mind. Consultants should not randomly seek information just for the purpose of seeking information and pray that a purpose will reveal itself down the road. Asking a client to gather information can take up precious time and resources, so consultants should balance need and effort required.

Sometimes avoiding fishing is not as easy as it seems, especially in cases where strategic or operational problems may not be readily visible. To avoid the pitfall of fishing, a consultant should use a structured methodology for attacking the client problem statement, and the methodology should be connected to end results and either prove or disprove the hypotheses as much as possible. For example, in analyzing back office operations for a client, one may want to use a structured methodology for looking at people, processes, and systems. One may look at the roles people are playing, document the workflows people are using, and examine the computer support for various paper handling steps. To illustrate how the boundaries of data collection must be clearly understood, suppose during a back office operations assessment the client executive determines that salary information of the workers analyzed will be off-limits to the consultant. At that point, the consultant may want to state that any potential problems about whether a client's workers are paid competitively, which potentially affects worker quality and effectiveness, will be beyond the scope of the consulting analysis.

Another way to avoid the pitfall of fishing is for the consultant to ask for information in a layered way. That is, before diving deep into numerous areas of investigation, a consultant can ask for broad, easy-to-access information first. If the first layer of information reveals a potential problem in the client's current approach, a consultant can then ask for more detailed information.

So all in all, hunter instincts are good traits for consultants to have, but fisher tendencies need to either be watched carefully or avoided entirely.

Takeaway Exercise: If you are a practitioner preparing

for an assessment, take a moment to examine your game plan for executing. Identify elements of the assessment that do not clearly map back to the problem statement for the engagement and might fall into the realm of fishing. Consider seeking input from a peer or manager as to whether that type of fishing should be of concern.

7
GIVING SIMPLE OPINIONS VERSUS PRACTICING CONSULTING SCIENCE

Here are a few examples of how one might provide consulting support for a portion of a client project. The examples are based on real-world tactics taken by consultants who are posed with the problem of characterizing the threat of competitive entry by another company.

Consultant #1's characterization:

- The threat of competitive entry is moderate

The characterization is okay. If one reads between the lines here, one might presume that the person is saying that competition will neither be heavy nor light. Based on microeconomics-type conventions, the former case could mean that there are between two and three competitors and the potential for price wars. In the latter case, only one competitor and sales might go relatively unchallenged. The characterization is very general and leaves a lot to be desired.

A better characterization might be:

- Competitive entry may occur within two to five years by one known competitor already operating in another region

This characterization gives more specific details and timeframes provided there are details to back up the claims.

Here are some thoughts on an assessment which is also

backed by facts ("consulting science") to support the claim. When a consultant uses hard, quantifiable facts, the arguments and characterization become much less subject to potential challenges by others that results are biased by any personal opinions of the consultant.

Consultant #2's characterization:

- Competitive entry may be expected by one competitor, likely two or more years out.
- Current market structure is mostly a duopoly, indicating moderate price pressure potential.
- The perspective on longer timeframe for competitor entry is based on regulatory requirements concerning X, Y, and Z; of these the first two are relevant to client.
- The perspective on timeframe for competitive entry is based on public capital and operating expenditures filed in public financial documents and benchmarking of these current expenditures against comparables.
- Subjectively, the business structure that the competitor is using has a high failure rate.
- Historical entry of competitor is X, Y, and Z, and if history repeats itself where competitive entry does occur earlier than foreseen, competitive entry will likely look like A from marketing and sales perspective, B from a technical perspective, and C from a financial resources perspective.
- Entry scenarios are further substantiated by the number of retail points and the form factor of product used by the company's direct competitor and substitute players in other markets.

Tea leaf reading in consulting engagements can be challenging. But sometimes tea leaf reading needs to be done, especially when stakes are high. All said, there are methods that consultants can use to better support their clients, as opposed to dispensing simple advice. The latter I dare not call consulting.

Takeaway Exercise: Examine the problem statement for an engagement you are working on or managing.

Assess the high-stakes questions and where more science may be needed to support key recommendations.

8
MANAGING PROGRESS TO GOALS

One of the earliest lessons for me in management consulting had to do with getting a client organization to move. I don't know if there is a formal name for the approach, but for the purposes here, I'll call it "managing progress to goals."

The essence of this approach begins with the consultant working with the client organization to establish one or more measureable goals and then reporting on actual performance and gaps. Let's say a goal is to create $5.5 million in annual revenue for a new start-up initiative: $500,000 in the first quarter, $1.0 million in the second quarter, $2.0 million in the third quarter, and $2.0 million in the fourth quarter. The consultant then works with the client to put a regular measurement system in place, say monthly. Suppose that by the end of the first quarter, the client has only achieved 15% of the goal. The consultant should be working with the manager owning the revenue to report not only the numeric gap in performance, but also a diagnostic of why things are off track. This should be from both quantitative and qualitative perspectives.

Although the technique may seem obvious, in many situations one may be diagnosing problems or setting up operations for things that happen below a corporate-level or business unit-level where measurements and monitoring may not fully exist. Some example situations where measurements may not be readily available include setting up new business structures (e.g., new business line) or bypassing old business structures (e.g., where old methods are too cumbersome or bureaucratic).

Other than the primary goal of trying to help the client, the flip side of this is that the consultant is trying to manage expectations. One can't start a project and then six months later show up and simply report to executive management that the goal wasn't met by the business unit or functional area management. Progress to goal (and gap) reporting is needed every step of the way, along with mid-course control and corrections. In this way, the consultant also separates the aspects of proper management control from management's ability to execute.

Takeaway Exercise: Assess an engagement you are working on or managing. Determine whether you have a good dashboard for assessing progress relative to goals.

9
BROADEN PERSPECTIVES USING OTHERS OR THIRD PARTIES

Getting different perspectives can be very helpful for many business activities, whether related to strategy, innovation, or operations. And sometimes actual assistance from other parties may be desired or necessary. While the third-party might be an outside consultant, it could also be other organizationally close or distant people within the firm. An advisor, a vendor representative, or a peer-level person within another company may also be involved.

My guess is that it unnatural for people to look for outside help. Inertia often biases people to act within traditional boundaries. If an organization is currently operating without getting outside perspectives, it can take too much energy and effort to look elsewhere. So rather than prescribe when you should seek input or help from a third-party, instead consider some situations when you might benefit from doing so. Some example situations:

- You want to invest in a new effort. It can be hard to run company while changing direction or simultaneously building a new capability.
- The core team needs to get perspectives on other companies and trends, both inside and outside the focus industry.

- The organization needs to evolve its culture and DNA.
- Management wants to recover or restart a previously failed effort.
- A business unit needs to plug a gap, perhaps leveraging resources from another area within the company.
- Management wants to mediate or facilitate a program or business initiative, requiring new cross-functional activities.
- Executives want to signal substantive actions and investment to outside world or other areas of company.
- Management wants to audit a current project or business processes.
- Organization needs to fill a management gap.

Takeaway Exercise: Take a moment to think freely and set aside thinking about logistics or costs. Where would it be most helpful to get a new perspective? Or think of an area where you've never gotten an outsider's perspective? Where are these areas? Discuss your findings with colleagues.

10
THREE PROTOTYPICAL STYLES OF CONSULTING

In 2009 I was debating my thoughts on how a particular consulting engagement should come together. Sometimes to address a problem statement there may be a number of "ways to skin a cat" and get an engagement team to gel. In this particular case, my feeling was that the engagement approach could shift towards one of the three prototypes:

- **Research-centric consulting** – Detailed frameworks from brand management, business strategy, pricing, statistics, finance, etc. often form the backbone of the approach. The consulting team can piece together a storyboard that tees up hypotheses, finds supporting or disconfirming evidence, and builds a case towards strategic options and recommendations. In this type of consulting, domain and industry expertise are somewhat less critical because a structured problem solving methodology underpins the approach. In terms of situational use, this type of consulting may be prevalent in cases where a client lacks a rigorous approach or in cases where new businesses are being explored but where there are few role models.
- **Expertise-centric consulting** – In this type of consulting, a consultant brings to the table either or

both domain and industry knowledge. For example, has the consultant helped to launch a mobile virtual operator before? Or does the consultant specialize in an expertise niche such as optimizing cross-media spending for mega brands using econometric approaches? Or has a consultant worked in brand litigation and expert witness cases related to marketing? Can the consultant bring forth an engagement structure that has been tested before in another situation?

- **Facilitative consulting** – In this style, the consultant brings value to the table by bringing personal experiences and skills. The consultant may also bring third-party perspectives which also add value. But the real value is in weaving together the consulting team and client team to solve the customer problem statement. For example, the consultant may conduct client interviews with separate functional groups within the client organization and with client customers. The consultant then organizes and normalizes information from the various interviews and develops strategic options and frameworks that can be used in iterative client meetings to refine and finalize strategy. The facilitative consulting approach is akin to combining the skills of a general manager with a project manager.

The prototypical styles of consulting that I describe above are not mutually exclusive. Often, engagements will have multiple aspects, although I've seen engagements that are predominantly one prototype. I think that many consultants, general managers, and project manager types could benefit by understanding the consulting prototypes better. In some sense, they are like the primary colors for setting the tone and customizing a consulting engagement.

Takeaway Exercise: Consider an engagement that you are about to start. Assess to what extent your approach will incorporate the three areas of research, expertise, and facilitation. Should the approach be strengthened in one or more of these areas?

SECTION TWO: CONSULTING TECHNIQUES

11
IN CONSULTING THE PROCESS IS AN ESSENTIAL PART OF THE DELIVERABLE

Situation for Consultant #1:

- Client needs help in determining business strategy and writing business plan for its Board.
- Consultant follows traditional MBA frameworks by performing 3Cs (Customer, Competition, Company), Porter's Five Forces and competitive advantage, etc. to research and analyze the best way for client to move forward.
- Consultant uses structured frameworks for outlining and documenting the tactics and logistics for pursuing the business (e.g., marketing 4Ps, traditional business plan outlines).
- Consultant prepares full financial proformas: balance sheet, income statement, cash flow statement, and notes.
- Consultant writes business plan to spec.
- Consultant delivers written business plan to client.
- Consultant invoices $40,000.
- Client ends up being lukewarm about the deliverable.

Situation for Consultant #2 (differences in bold):

- Client needs help in determining business strategy and writing business plan for its Board.
- **Consultant sets up engagement timeframe and governance structure with consulting team and client leads, extended resources for all key workstreams, and steering/approval committee.**
- Consultant follows traditional MBA frameworks by performing 3Cs (Customer, Competition, Company), Porter's Five Forces and competitive advantage, etc. to research and analyze the best way for client to move forward.
- **Consultant sets up workshops and strategy sessions with the executive team, key functional managers, etc.**
- Consultant uses structured frameworks for outlining and documenting the tactics and logistics for pursuing the business (e.g., marketing 4Ps, traditional business plan outlines).
- **Consultant sets up regular review meetings and working sessions with client to review best practices, evaluate options, and refine and revise strategy.**
- Consultant prepares full financial proformas: balance sheet, income statement, cash flow statement, and notes.
- **Consultant sets up working sessions to familiarize client with models, align financials with chart of accounts for client, get client input, and educate client about industry benchmarks.**
- Consultant writes business plan to spec.
- **Consultant involves client with interim drafts and presentations and gets organizational buy-in**
- Consultant delivers written business plan to client **(largely same as before)**.
- Consultant invoices **$250,000**.
- **Client is very happy and ends up getting multimillion-dollar business moving forward through Board and project launched.**

Business plan without client buy-in processes… $40,000.
Business plan with client buy-in processes… priceless.

Takeaway Exercise: Present the structure of an engagement to a peer or manager. Ask them to review the engagement process with an eye toward how to involve the company organization most effectively (e.g., in terms of governance, kickoff, meetings, workshops, creation and review of materials, and closeout). Refine the process and communicate with the company organization as appropriate.

12
WHAT A SAMPLE MANAGEMENT CONSULTING DELIVERABLE LOOKS LIKE

It is relatively easy to find papers, articles, and magazine publications written by those at management consulting firms. While these publications can be excellent sources of information, they tend shed light on the thought leadership, research base, and marketing aspects of consulting firms. For those that are trying to learn about consulting firms and the presentations they produce for clients to facilitate strategy and change, there is comparatively less public information that represents a concrete, traditional management consulting deliverable. In a large part, this is because many consulting engagements involve confidential relationships between the consulting firm and the client, and disclosure is not permitted.

In this chapter, I reference a number of examples of consulting deliverables (Note: most are public-sector deliverables). While not universally true, there are two themes that are widely used in consulting presentations:

- The presentations reflect how best practice consulting should be driven by facts and a scientific approach to the fullest extent possible. For example, it is very common from presentations to contain both benchmarking information and comprehensive analysis from numerous perspectives.

- In my opinion, the best presentations implement "key takeaway-style" as opposed to "topic-style" titling of slides. Key takeaway-style titling is a method that I did not have much exposure to before entering consulting back in the late 1990s, and to this day it is still a method that I infrequently see in corporate environments. See the figures below as examples.

Key Takeaway-Style

Delivery strategy will be based on core team of 25 FTEs with augmentation to address different situations

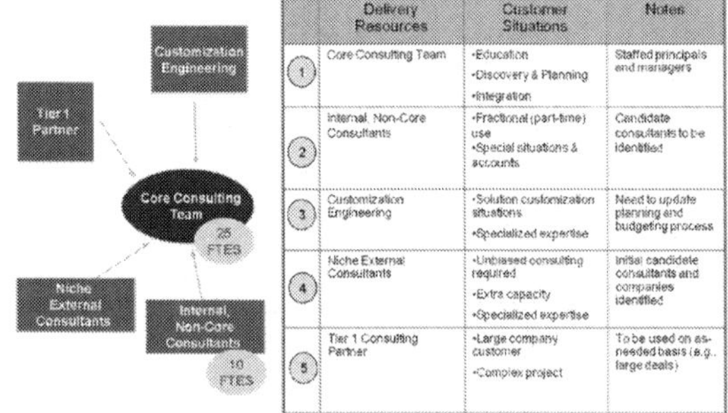

	Delivery Resources	Customer Situations	Notes
1	Core Consulting Team	•Education •Discovery & Planning •Integration	Staffed principals and managers
2	Internal, Non-Core Consultants	•Fractional (part-time) use •Special situations & accounts	Candidate consultants to be identified
3	Customization Engineering	•Solution customization situations •Specialized expertise	Need to update planning and budgeting process
4	Niche External Consultants	•Unbiased consulting required •Extra capacity •Specialized expertise	Initial candidate consultants and companies identified
5	Tier 1 Consulting Partner	•Large company customer •Complex project	To be used on as-needed basis (e.g., large deals)

Downloadable figure available at: http://steveshuconsulting.com/2000/01/download-figures-the-consulting-apprenticeship

Topic-Style

Delivery strategy

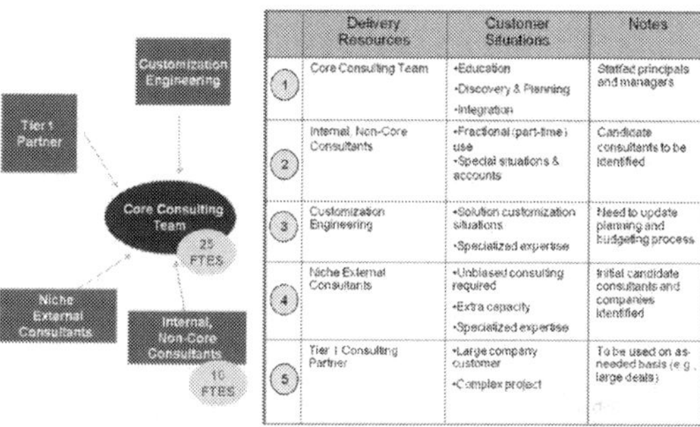

	Delivery Resources	Customer Situations	Notes
1	Core Consulting Team	•Education •Discovery & Planning •Integration	Staffed principals and managers
2	Internal, Non-Core Consultants	•Fractional (part-time) use •Special situations & accounts	Candidate consultants to be identified
3	Customization Engineering	•Solution customization situations •Specialized expertise	Need to update planning and budgeting process
4	Niche External Consultants	•Unbiased consulting required •Extra capacity •Specialized expertise	Initial candidate consultants and companies identified
5	Tier 1 Consulting Partner	•Large company customer •Complex project	To be used on as-needed basis (e.g., large deals)

Downloadable figure available at: http://steveshuconsulting.com/2000/01/download-figures-the-consulting-apprenticeship

Notice how the title for the first slide reads, "Delivery strategy will be based on core team of 25 FTEs with augmentation based on situation." Even if one can't read the detailed figures in the slides, one can read just the titles of the slides to get the overall executive storyline. The title for the first slide makes it clear what the consultant wanted the audience to take away as the key message. It turns out that the primary focus for this slide was to support the financial budgeting process, and so the consultant wanted to point out 25 FTEs as the resource need for the core team. Now suppose that instead of key takeaway-style that topic-style titling was used. See how the second slide reads, "Delivery strategy." In this case one has to read the entire slide to try to extract the key message. And the key message that the audience takes away might end up being different from what the consultant wanted them to take away. In this case, one audience member might first look at the box on the left that reads, "Tier 1 Partner." They might conclude that the company needs to immediately work on its Tier 1 Partner relationship. Another audience member might look at the five types of delivery resources and start to conclude that customer situation analysis scenarios are the most important thing to focus on. While these may all be good things to discuss, the consultant risks losing both attention of the audience and focus on the end goal.

Now it is important to caveat this discussion by mentioning that the presentation deliverable is only one type of deliverable by a consulting firm. It is also worth mentioning that it is easy to look at a deliverable and completely miss the process aspect of how consulting deliverables may be generated. The process may be equally, if not more important than the deliverable, and the process varies by consulting firm.

Takeaway Exercise: Broaden your perspectives by looking at sample deliverables from a number of consulting firms listed at http://steveshuconsulting.com/2010/01/chap12-consulting-apprenticeship

13
USING THE SEEDING AND FACILITATING TECHNIQUE

One technique that I tend to use a lot in management meetings and consulting engagements involves the use of two types of slides. The first I call the Seeding Technique; the second the Facilitating Technique. The purpose of these slides is often to help the management team get aligned and make critical business decisions.

The objectives of the Seeding slide are to articulate the general problem statement area and enable the management team to voice issues on specific areas within that vicinity. Note that in these situations, the exact problem statement may not be known or agreed upon. As such, it is often useful to research and include some frameworks or metaphors on the Seeding slide that enable the management team to warm up and express issues from multiple perspectives.

The objectives of the Facilitating slide are to help the management team move forward and begin the dialogue of exploring potential solutions to the problem at hand. It is often helpful to do some research on answers that can help seed the solution-exploration process. Research can take the form of best practices, case studies, academic solutions, etc. The meeting leader must work hard to apply their best facilitation skills on this slide – when to use open-ended questioning, when to analyze, and when to steer to closure.

The examples below depict what Seeding and Facilitating slides might look like in a workshop setting to help a consulting organization reposition itself.

Seeding Slide

We are losing deals because our consulting business focuses too much on technology only.

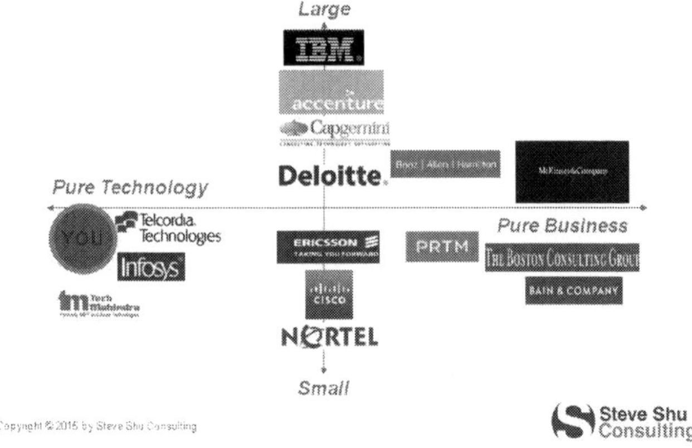

Facilitating Slide

How should we reposition ourselves in the consulting landscape?

Area	Key Questions
Market Opportunity	Where are we missing the boat?
Skill Versus Scale	•What do we do well? •What don't we do well?
Offensive Versus Defensive	•Which is it? •Why?
Support Existing Business	•What should the priority be? •What are the risks?
Grow Independent Business	•What are the benefits? •What are the dangers?
Key Goals	•What does success look like? •What keeps us awake at night?

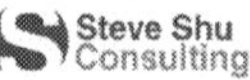

Downloadable figures available at:
http://steveshuconsulting.com/2000/01/download-figures-

the-consulting-apprenticeship

Takeaway Exercise: Think of a challenge facing your business or client where first setting a baseline and then having an open-ended discussion might help. See if you can structure one or two slides to apply the Seeding and Facilitating technique.

14
PAINTING THE ENDS OF THE SPECTRUM

One technique I've found very useful when facilitating a diverse group of folks is "painting the ends of the spectrum."

Here are a couple of examples:

- **Trying to hone in on a direction related to strategy** – In discussions with a client, framing the discussion by saying something to the effect of, "On the one spectrum, we can focus on simply reviewing the documents to make sure all parties understand. This will require a fairly short period of time. On the other end of the spectrum, we can work towards developing a common solution. Such an approach will require more time and strategy planning on our end." This can be followed up by either the question, "Where do you think we should be aiming for on the spectrum?" Alternatively depending on the bias you feel acceptable for the situation, you may indicate, "I think the former end of the spectrum is preferable. That said, what do you think?"
- **Attempting to gauge direction on customer preference** – The technique can often be used in primary market research or sales situations. Here you may ask, "On the one end of the spectrum you can

> have a solution that covers X, Y, and Z, and will, for a premium fee, meet your end needs of being able to sleep at night. On the other end of the spectrum, you can have a narrower solution that has smaller out-of-pocket fees and may require greater coordination and integration on your part. Which direction do you prefer and why?"

Painting the ends of the spectrum works in many situations, particularly if complexity is somewhat linear (e.g., moving from simple to complex). In some cases, you may find it useful to paint other colors in the middle of the spectrum too. I tend to find that this latter situation works well when supported with visuals.

Takeaway Exercise: Set a goal to use this technique in at least one conversation or group meeting in the coming week.

15
KILLER PICTURES AND THE QUESTION "SO WHAT?"

Two characteristics of a great consultant are making things understandable and actionable. And when it comes to deliverables, such as presentations, here are two things to aspire to:

- **Create The Killer Picture** – A picture is worth a thousand words. Summarizing a complex concept in a structured, scientific, and visual way can be invaluable in consulting engagements. Successful consultants must prove wrong the saying that "consultants use their client's watch to tell them the time." Consultants are on the right track when they can synthesize analysis into a crisp picture and get the client to react with something to the effect of "that's really important and something I didn't know about myself."
- **Answer the Question "So What?"** – Creating fancy pictures is not enough. Without bottom line and prescriptive messages for analysis, consultants and managers may be flooding their audiences with information and clouding the purpose. Sometimes adding scorecard or ranking information to charts can complement important prescriptions, like "Client needs to focus on improving six red flagged areas

which cost the client $X per annum in above average churn."

The combination of creating killer pictures and answering the so what question is a gold standard in consulting.

Takeaway Exercise: Many consultants set a goal to create at least one killer picture each day. Try to build a habit over the next two weeks. Each day create a killer picture for either personal or professional use. It could be as simple as sketching your thoughts on a napkin. Make sure to answer the "So What" question.

16
THE WORKSHOP AS PART OF STRATEGY CONSULTING

Client workshops are elements that I have often seen as part of consulting engagements, but I have found little written information about them. I have often set up workshops for engagements related to business or marketing strategy, but workshops are not limited to these scenarios.

Suppose a client is looking to enter a new business, and they want to determine a strategy for entering the business in terms of business structure, channel structure, pricing methods, division of operational responsibilities, etc. A consultant may structure a workshop where key elements are discussed in a management or executive setting with a client:

- Case studies of competitors.
- Case studies of comparable companies in related sectors.
- Consultant research and points of view on client issue area.
- Client point of view and prior experiences.
- Industry trends, unsolved problems, and innovative solutions.

By engaging in a workshop, the consultant helps to level set with the client and to ensure that many points of view are brought in, especially to encourage ”blue sky“ thinking. Note that the workshop can be designed to set up a fact-based foundation and facilitate structured discussions. When designed properly, the structure helps consultants from giving and clients from receiving shallow advice.

Note that other frameworks can be weaved into the workshop structure. For example, suppose the consultant has specific methodologies for assessing whether a product development process can be improved and that this methodology covers four distinct areas. The workshop can be carefully designed to weave around those four areas.

The workshop needs to have specific goals in order to be effective. In some cases, the workshop may be a first step to get the client thinking about where they think priorities should be for their business. In other cases, the desired outcome of the workshop may be for the consultant to help the client with two to three focus areas that become evident during the workshop. Other outcomes might include performing financial analysis of different business scenarios and ideas generated during the workshop. The possibilities for workshops within consulting engagements are endless.

Takeaway Exercise: Seek out both an opportunity to outline the structure for a workshop and review a workshop designed by another consultant.

17
THE NICKEL TOUR

One of the less glamorous management consulting projects I remember hearing about a number of years ago was in the turkey processing business. That discussion reminded me of the wide variety of unusual situations consultants face when assigned to new projects, and the discussion prompted me to write the content for this chapter.

Now in many operations projects, key goals are to improve business dimensions such as:

- average throughput
- inventory backlog
- peak capacity
- quality
- cycle-time
- cost
- risk and failure points

Companies often have many business processes in place. Sometimes there may be a manageable set of predominant process flows, but then there can be zillions of microflows. One way for a consultant to get grounded in a situation in the face of complexity is to go on a "nickel tour" with the client.

In the case of the management consultant I met with, the goal of current project was to reduce the number of injuries, to increase safety, and reduce lawsuits in the processing plants of one of the big turkey producers. The automated equipment in certain sectors of the meat business can be quite scary and potentially dangerous for operators. Not for the faint-hearted for sure; some of the equipment can separate meat from bone of entire animals in matters of a few seconds.

So on the first day the consultant arrives on the scene, one of the plant workers hands the consultant a pair of rubber boots to go on a nickel tour of the plant. I don't think the tour was of the slaughterhouse, but one can imagine that the scene was not everything a recent business school graduate dreams of visiting as a consultant.

In nickel tours that I've taken, the client has walked me through the back office operations, introduced me to sales personnel, asked me to sit in on calls with customer service representatives, attend information technology user sessions, etc. The purpose of the tour was to provide me with a ground-floor view of what happens in the business and an opportunity to ask initial questions. The nickel tour helped to compress a complex view of the business into one short experience. The experience can serve as a very valuable source for initial information; you may see large piles of inventory, frazzled or distressed workers, and disorganized workspaces. As a consultant, you may also meet people that can serve as useful sources of information later in an engagement.

On the flipside, a consultant needs to be wary of "stage plays." This is a case where the nickel tour is not a real tour of operations, but a case where someone within the client operations has dressed up the situation to be different or better than it really is on a day-to-day basis.

In any case, make sure to think about giving or getting a nickel tour in a consulting relationship. Although it is not always possible or desirable in some cases to get a nickel tour, this can really help consultants get a concrete feel for the business at hand.

Takeaway Exercise: Provided that it is consistent with the engagement, seek out an opportunity to get a nickel tour. The tour could even be more on paper versus physical, such as a walkthrough of a sales presentation that is used by a company with its customers.

18
BOTTLENECK RELIEF TECHNIQUE

When thrust into a situation where either resources are constrained, there are competing management choices, or paths forward are unclear, I often find a bottleneck relief technique useful to consider.

At its core, bottleneck relief is used for addressing production and operations problems. Usually I approach these types of problems from one of two angles. One angle is more technical and can include diagramming out process flows and calibrating measures according to things like Little's Law, where average inventory is approximately equal to average throughput time average cycle time. The second angle is more qualitative, and it may be done in a facilitative means through interviews and collaborative problem solving with client management. For example, performance issues could be evidenced where inventory (e.g., backlog, incomplete jobs, unresolved decisions, open sales leads) is piling up. When things are piling up, they are also likely taking a long time to get through the process, since per Little's Law, inventory and cycle time are directly related when resources are held constant. Let's take a closer look at the second angle.

For example, suppose a startup is trying to figure out how to ramp up sales from its first deals, where its first deals are largely non-repeatable because they were unique and early in the learning curve. Suppose you have one hour with client management. How might you help to tease out how where to start looking for improvements?

A bottleneck relief technique might focus on finding out where one gets the biggest bang for the buck in terms of making an operational change. Here I might explore with the client if they had additional resources (e.g., people, dollars, time), which of the following would ultimately result in more sales throughput:

- **Refining Strategy** – This might involve breaking the customer base into segments. Which segments have the lowest-hanging fruit in terms of sales opportunities? What kind of marketing and sales material is each segment getting? If there was a choice to improve the marketing collateral or sales processes for one of the segments, which one should be chosen? Are there backlogs in the system (e.g., uncalled sales lead prospects) that are indicative of bottlenecks?
- **Building Scalability** - In many startup situations, executives may make the first sales, but as the organization grows they may have problems transferring knowledge on how those sales were made. Would it be helpful to have someone shadow key executives to distill the sales processes and real value propositions that various customers are buying?
- **Adjusting Product and Simplifying Purchase Processes** - How much can the customer purchase process be improved by simplifying product functionality or choices? Is there a way that we can get people to sample or experience the product before purchase?

The bottleneck relief technique is important to have in one's arsenal of tools and can especially be used in facilitative situations where the organization has substantial tacit knowledge. The method can also be good when troubleshooting a problem that cuts across functional areas.

Takeaway Exercise: Think of a specific company area where output and quality of outcomes are issues. To apply the bottleneck relief method, first assess where inventory or backlog is building up, capacity is

constrained in promoting quality output, and cycle or turnaround time is longer than desired. Brainstorm options for changing processes. To what extent do some of your options seem promising?

19
USING TRIANGULATION

The concept of "triangulation" seems to be something used in the investment banking and management consulting areas, but it is something that I have found used much less frequently when working with operating companies. I define triangulation as a systematic process of using multiple methods to gather a range of quantitative estimates for an unknown or debatable value.

A classic example of how one could triangulate the value of a company is as follows:

- Estimate the value of company using a multiples method of company value based on revenue (e.g., value of company equals 2.5 times revenue or a market comparables multiplier).
- Estimate the value of company using a multiples method of company value based on profits (e.g., value of company equals 6.0 times EBITDA or a market comparables multiplier).
- Use discounted cash flow (DCF) method (e.g., use current and projected financials to value the company based on the free cash flows thrown off by the business).

Once you have done this, layout all of the estimations on a "football field" type chart. Here the horizontal axis is the method used, so there are three points signifying multiples method #1, multiples method #2, and DCF method. The vertical axis is the valuation of the company. The plots could be floating bars with the high and low end of the bars signifying the high and low estimates for each valuation technique. Sometimes a company or practitioner may have methods of weighing one technique more than the others. Come up with your final range of estimates for the low, high, and average based on the football field.

The figure below highlights another example of triangulation motivated by an engagement involving wireless spectrum valuation. The basic idea is that my team used three methods to get the range of potential dollar values for each wireless spectrum property. The chart below is the summary chart that ties the results of separate analyses together. The first method of valuation on the left (historic comparables) involved looking at past government auctions for similar properties and coming up with high, low, and in-between values. The second method of valuation (economic model) used a statistical regression model trained on a priori auction conditions (e.g., number of bidders, amount of money ante) and ex-post results (e.g., property values), and here we basically used the model to predict what might be the outcome of a new, unseen auction. The third model (financial metrics) basically took a look at recent market transactions (e.g., outright asset sales) or values imputed by the stock market value of wireless-heavy companies (e.g., by taking enterprise value and normalizing by spectrum holding amount).

Triangulation Example

The recommended maximum auction bid for wireless spectrum is $0.20 / MHz * POP

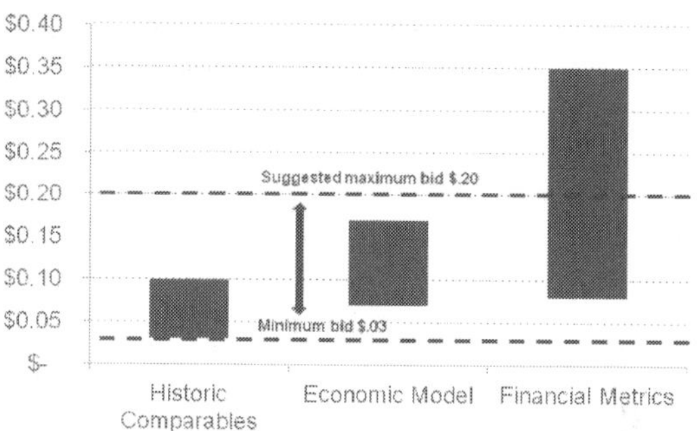

Downloadable figure available at: http://steveshuconsulting.com/2000/01/download-figures-the-consulting-apprenticeship

When one plots these three different valuation methods on the same chart, it becomes possible to "triangulate" and see what a competitive values for the wireless properties might be. We basically added two horizontal lines to depict the expected minimum amount of money to pay to be in the game and also the maximum amount of money that should be spent (e.g., based on balance sheet of company and financial capacity).

As some final thoughts, triangulation can also be valuable in areas outside of valuation. For example, these methods can be used when trying to estimate a prospective channel partner's product demand, job loading on a workforce, or the potential penetration and growth rate of a competitor in a particular market. Although triangulation can be a bit of a mundane topic, it can be a powerful friend. It takes some conscious effort to make triangulation use a habit. It also takes some creativity to come at things from different angles, but keeping on your toes is a good thing.

Takeaway Exercise: Work with a peer or colleague to try to find another example of using triangulation. See if you

can identify a new technique that you've not used before.

20
SPRING CLEANING AND GETTING OVER HUMPS

The next technique is something that I've seen a number of operating companies and management consulting firms use. The technique never had a formal name, but I call it the Spring Cleaning technique. The Spring Cleaning technique consists of an executive- or management-level meeting to talk about the business in breadth, capture issues (no-holds barred), rank issues, strategize, and divide and conquer.

The basic value of a Spring Cleaning management team meeting is as follows:

- **The meeting forces people to think proactively.** While management may have regular weekly management meetings, it becomes easy to become caught up in the day-to-day grind and push off things that people don't have time for but know are important.
- **The manager that oversees the functional line roles has an opportunity to reset expectations and goals.** The psychology of starting fresh can re-energize the organization.
- **Involvement of a consultant can provide a third-party perspective, and in some cases, extra project bandwidth to overcome organizational inertia.**

> The consultant may be expected to work with all of the parties above to prepare information in advance, facilitate meeting discussions, organize issues and action items, and develop a project structure for making and tracking progress. The consultant can essentially act as right-hand person to the sponsoring manager.

In the Spring Cleaning meetings that I have worked on, typical meetings may last a couple of days. The first day of meetings my involve level-setting and brainstorming on strategies. Between these days, the consultant may work to organize the notes, data, or perform analyses. The next day of meetings may be spent working through the high points, prioritizing, and identifying more detailed next steps.

While situations vary, the consultant may be retained as a both a project manager for the larger effort and as specialist to work with a specific functional group to implement change. In these change management situations, the organization may be trying to get over humps or change course while running the business. The value of the project management aspect should not be underestimated.

Takeaway Exercise: Spring comes once a year. Schedule an annual Spring Cleaning session, even if you can only afford a short session.

SECTION THREE: CONSULTING MASTERY

21
EIGHT SECRET WEAPONS OF THE MODERN CONSULTANT

In addition to focusing on specifics related to the practice of consulting, it's often useful to take a step back and examine the larger picture. In this chapter, I've tied things together into a framework of secret weapons of the modern consultant. Secret weapons are a spectrum of tactics and skill areas. While some may be used widely, they are often passed through mentorship or apprenticeship in bits and pieces. A modern consultant is a professional that can work in dynamic industries, operate within multiple types of consulting organizations (e.g., niche, large traditional), and has experience as both an operating manager and an advisor.

So here are eight secret weapons of the modern consultant (arranged roughly in order from foundational to more advanced):

1. **Problem Statement Articulation Skills** – This skill requires a consultant to define the boundaries of a scope of work. Implicit to this is being able to define what decisions points need to be met and the managerial significance of the issue at hand. Because the organization is preparing to commit resources to investigating a problem, this is core to getting started. To see more detail on this subject, see Chapter 3:

Articulating and Rearticulating Problem Statements.

2. **Structured Problem-Solving Skills and Industry Knowledge** – Skills with structured approaches may be developed by learning key frameworks, such as the popularized McKinsey MECE approach, which refers to "mutually exclusive, collective exhaustive" (Rasiel 1999). Skills can also be gleaned from thinking about how one would practice consulting science versus giving simple advice (see Chapter 7: Giving Simple Opinions Versus Practicing Consulting Science). Aspects of industry knowledge come through experience and specialization, and can also be augmented by reading trade websites or publications and participating in trade events or groups.
3. **Engagement Management Mastery** – This skill ties together problem statement, structured approaches, and industry knowledge, but goes further. Mastery includes both synthesizing the resources that will solve the problem statement for the engagement and managing the relationship between consultant, client management, and the client executive sponsor. For more info on the engagement management topic, see Chapter 2: Engagement Management is the Essence of Management Consulting.
4. **Interpersonal, Facilitation, and Leadership Skills** – Interpersonal and leadership skills are pretty well documented in other areas. One of my favorite foundational books on leadership is *The Leadership Challenge* (Kouzes and Posner 2012). On facilitation skills, I have seen less documentation on the subject in a concise format. Facilitation skills are especially important because they help a professional in cases where authority does not exist and where influence must be used to achieve management goals. Also see Chapter 5: Client Facilitation Skills.
5. **Storytelling and Executive Analysis Skills** – At least two core frames of thinking come to mind, when I think about this subject. The first frame is best illustrated by how one ties together presentation slides in a storyboard using "key takeaway style" versus

"topic style" titling as described in Chapter 12: What a Sample Management Consulting Deliverable Looks Like. The second key frame is driving towards answering the "So What?" questions along the way in an analysis presentation as described in Chapter 15: Killer Pictures and the Question "So What?". If I had to add an additional reference on true storytelling, I would add a book by screenwriter Robert McKee called *Story*, particularly with his treatment of events and how story values are "universal qualities of human experience that may shift from positive to negative, or negative to positive, from one moment to the next" (McKee 1997).

6. **Adaptation Skills** – When I think of developing adaptation skills, I think of developing skills that improve behavior and communications skills in the moment (for example leveraging improv concepts). I also think being able to change one's frame of thinking with concepts such as, "there are no sacred cows," is an important tool to have at one's disposal. The mindset of continuously seeking out better ideas, better ways of describing things, and new approaches is healthy and powerful.
7. **Business Development and Management Skills** – Consulting services sales and marketing are unique topics. Too often people fall into the trap of buying any type of sales or marketing book. For example, some books are focused more on products or solutions to non-confidential problems. On the other hand, reading books like *Rain Making* (Harding 2008), *Creating Rainmakers* (Harding 1998), and *Winning the Professional Services Sale* (McLaughlin 2009) are some of the best investments that one can make because services related to confidential solutions are different animals. For the management of consulting firms, one of my go-to references is *Managing the Professional Services Firm* (Maister 1997).
8. **Forecasting and Envisioning Skills** – The eighth secret weapon is more elusive. Some of it involves developing systems thinking such as described by

Peter Senge and his book, *The Fifth Discipline* (Senge 2006). Some of it may come from understanding innovation frameworks and processes better. For example, Roberto Verganti has a great book called *Design Driven Innovation*, which emphasizes innovation of meanings versus technological progress (Verganti 2009). Or it might be by applying social responsibility concepts. For me, I see three prototypes of people that develop the eighth secret weapon: those that have innate talent and vision already, those that develop such skills by mastering a craft or a practice area, and those that heavily use their networks to develop insights into the future.

So there you have it. Eight secret weapons to further one's mastery of consulting.

Takeaway Exercise: Rate yourself on scale of 1 to 10 in the eight areas above. Set a concrete action plan for improving one of these areas during this year.

22 MANAGEMENT CONSULTING MANIFESTO

I am passionate about seeking better ways to practice business and management consulting. Writing down my views and values helps me become a better professional. Here is my manifesto:

- Do what's best for the client before the consulting firm.
- Lead and practice ethically.
- Love the client and commit fully or leave at the earliest, ethical moment.
- Like the arts, mastery of leadership and business excellence are worthy pursuits.
- Practice consulting and avoid dispensing shallow advice.
- Apply analytics, process, and problem-solving rigor as your strengths to enlighten and lead versus obfuscate.
- Strive to introduce and apply principles of sustainability and social good wherever possible.
- Recognize limitations of consultative methods wherever they may be; seek noble, clever, and pragmatic solutions.
- Mentor colleagues and clients as appropriate and seek

mentors to improve oneself.

- Pursue mastery of interpersonal and organizational communications; get clients as far as you can along the curve in terms of understanding, commitment, and resolve.
- Seek a balance between personal and business life that complements and strengthens one another.

I encourage you to write a manifesto to further build commitment toward your ideals.

Takeaway Exercise: Write a professional manifesto. Share (as widely as you feel comfortable) the manifesto with colleagues, your manager, your family, and the public.

23
SCHOOLS OF THOUGHT ON LAYING OUT OPTIONS OR MAKING RECOMMENDATIONS

I've seen two schools of thought in management consulting regarding styles of either 1) laying out options for clients or 2) making recommendations to clients. Perhaps this will be a debate never fully resolved. Note that by highlighting these, I don't mean to imply that every engagement lends itself to one style or the other. For example, many implementation consulting engagements may be facilitation- or change management-oriented. On the other hand, strategy engagements often lead to decision-making crossroads where a pre-dominant school of thought might be desirable.

Now, sometimes people draw similarities between consultants and doctors in the way that advice should be dispensed. Now I'm no medical doctor, but most doctors I've seen lay out options for patients. They don't make decisions for them.

I am generally with that school of thought: consultants should lay out options for clients with the qualitative and quantitative tradeoffs. It is the client's responsibility to make a decision. In fact, some clients would be put off by an outsider telling them what they should do.

On the other hand, some clients believe that if consultants

work for them that the consultants should also state their own opinions on how to proceed. They may ask, "What would you do if you were in my shoes?"

This is delicate ground, but to be frank, I have at times stated my personal opinion while distancing it from the facts presented. I also make sure to caveat my personal opinion with any biases that I may have, while also emphasizing that I have kept personal biases out of the analysis given to the client.

In closing, if you are a consultant, you should definitely discuss the approach with your team and any guardrails that should be followed. It may also be helpful to have an explicit discussion with the client as to which style they would prefer.

Takeaway Exercise: Start a discussion with individuals on your consulting team about the subject of laying out options or making recommendations. See if everyone is on the same page in terms of approach. You might be surprised as to what you'll find out and learn.

24
SCHOOLS OF THOUGHT ON WHEN TO MAKE RECOMMENDATIONS

I run into quite a few people think of management consulting a lot more loosely than I do. I often run into people who say things like:

- "You should just go in there and start telling them what to do – go and consult."
- "Go and give them your advice."
- "I can do consulting. I can give them my expert advice."
- "So you tell them how to start wireless businesses?"

Although I've not described the context for these statements fully, these types of statements make me cringe. Why? Because people who say these things often presume that consultants start dispensing advice without understanding and gathering an inventory of a client's situation.

In some circumstances, maybe the consultant can jump right in to start making recommendations. For example, if a client is simply missing some basic fundamentals, like sales or operational reports and written contracts, one can dispense some advice from the start. But I tend to caution giving advice so early in a consulting relationship. I tend to prefer to share perspectives, as well as the factors or things I would need to investigate to either confirm or alter my initial read of the situation. This communicates to the client that I am not in the business of dispensing shallow advice. It also sets the frame for the consulting methodology that I am going to use to solve the problem at hand.

Now provided that a consultant is going to use a structured methodology for solving a client problem, at what point does the consultant make recommendations to the client?

My timing preference is based on the fact that clients ultimately have to live with proposed solutions. As such, I prefer the recommendation process to be more iterative. For example, on one project I may have to first gather competitive marketing information about mobile operators and benchmark my client against those competitors. The next step may be for me to outline the options that the client has to pursue to close the gaps (say increase efficiency of distribution points versus increase number and type of distribution points) along with the tradeoffs. As the final step, the client and I jointly work to decide the best path. By involving the client in the recommendations process, the client takes more ownership of the solution, and hence, the solution will tend to stick better.

On the other hand, another school of thought on timing is tied to size of the client organization and position within the industry. Using this school of thought for example, then if the client is a large Fortune 100, Tier 1 company, the consulting style should be more iterative. For smaller clients (e.g., middle-market companies), the thinking is that a consultant should take a stronger up-front stance on making recommendations and skipping a lot of the client facilitation processes.

I can see some benefits to the strong up-front approach as opposed to the iterative approach to the timing of recommendations:

- Consultant takes more control by initiative.
- Smaller companies do not have as many resources as larger companies and may need consultants to service as interim managers and not just as facilitators.
- Consultant may leave a stronger impression with the client by being strong up-front.

In summary, the choice of approach is a bit of a craft. By default, I would say that an iterative approach is better, especially if timelines and logistics permit. But the consultant needs to read the situation in terms of whether a client prefers a less iterative approach or and approach where the consultant makes strong recommendations more up-front.

Takeaway Exercise: Start a discussion with individuals on your consulting team about the subject of when to make recommendations to the client. Debate the tradeoffs of different approaches and formulate your own view of the world (you don't need to agree with mine).

25 AN IMPORTANT LESSON I'VE LEARNED FROM BUYERS OF CONSULTING SERVICES

There's been a good amount written on when to use management consultants. In some cases, consultants are used to help fix businesses that have run amuck. In other cases, consultants are used in cases when expertise is higher than that of existing employees. There are many different scenarios and arguments for using consultants. Companies should definitely examine the needs and tradeoffs for using consultants. Traditional tradeoffs include expertise, background in similar projects, knowledge retention, cost, incentives, organizational dependency issues, etc.

But I've learned something non-traditional and entrepreneurial from a number of buyers that deeply understand both how to use consultants and how to lead:

Many smart buyers of consulting services simply focus on making forward progress. Period. They focus on solving problems. Whether use of consultants is the best discount on future profits that a client has ever seen, the choice of whether to use consultants is less relevant than getting things done with a positive return.

As a long-time consultant, I am obviously somewhat biased. But I've been on the buyer side for consulting services too. Sometimes making progress is the most important goal, and satisficing trumps maximizing.

Takeaway Exercise: As you move up the mastery curve and deal with senior management, identify some at the top tier of professionals that you know and really respect. Really get to know them and learn about how they think. See if you can find something non-traditional about how these professionals think about consultants and when and where to use them.

26
ON WHETHER SELLING IS PRACTICING ONE'S PROFESSION

You can take the side of the argument that those who sell, such as partners in professional services firms and senior engineers, are indeed practicing their profession. On the other hand you may argue that such and such a person is no longer a practitioner because he or she now sells.

I tend to agree with the former of the two arguments, that those who sell are practicing their profession. In management consulting, the product is complex, and one really has to understand all aspects in order to sell. One needs to understand the methodologies that can be used, the importance of engagement structure, the value propositions, the variety of potential situations, the client organization and capability to change, potential pitfalls, what's going on in the industry, etc. The best people to sell consulting engagements are those that have been consultants, done many engagements (and are potentially involved in current engagements), and understand when and why a client should or should not use a consultant.

That said, I have found that many people have a hard time shifting gears from delivering engagements to selling engagements. For example, during the sales process, consultants newer to sales will want to ask about a lot of details, in effect trying to solve the client's problem during the presales process. But the purpose of the presales process is to establish credibility and rapport, identify the problems to be solved, create the link between the problem and the consulting engagement that will solve the problem, and sell the engagement. The presales process is not about solving the client's problem in a couple of meeting sessions. Granted, it is important to offer perspectives, opinions, industry data, and case studies during presales meetings. But those that have spent lots of time in delivery and little time in sales can lose sight of where one is in the sales process with a client prospect, and what questions absolutely need to be answered for the consultant to propose a scope of work and engagement structure.

Shifting focus from a delivery role to a sales role in consulting takes work. But because a large part of the sales role is to identify the problem statement and the best engagement structure, it can be a natural transition for many.

Takeaway Exercise: In consulting, learning about the sales and buying process is important if only to get a wider perspective on different value propositions and approaches. Take an inventory of when you last evaluated a consulting pitch, proposal, or opportunity. If you are a consultant, find opportunities to be involved with business development, read books on sales, or receive guidance from a mentor.

27
THE TAO OF TAKING APART CARS WITH ONE'S BARE HANDS

Business schools and management consulting firms provide their people with methodologies, best-in-class practices, historical case studies, scientific techniques, and the like as a foundation for their knowledge base. Usually there's a past experience, a past consulting project or something for consultants to draw on to solve a client's problem in the present.

But cases arise when a consultant in the field needs to solve a problem where it is almost impossible to draw from prior experiences or general frameworks. Problems of this flavor posed to me in the past include:

- Figuring out the optimum workflow for an outsourced function when the client is one of only two direct competitors in a closed industry where standard reference models are unknown.
- Sizing the business value and economic value of a human life for product development purposes.
- Valuing the price of a lease instrument that had never been created before, but that could be modeled as three separate instruments that had been created and valued before.
- Predicting a competitor's commercial bid (e.g., based

on imperfect information on their sales force structure, individual sales quotas, sales cycle times, number of deals).

I often liken the fuzziness of such situations to being posed the problem of having to take apart a locked car with one's bare hands, without the assistance of tools, machines of any kind, or prior knowledge of past practices. How might you take apart the car quickly if your life depended upon it?

Philosophically, one might try to breach the exterior of the car to get inside, where it might be easier to disassemble parts. One might break a window first, remove windshield wipers, use metal parts from the wipers as screwdrivers, unscrew pieces of the dashboard, and then try to move on from there. Note that there's no one right way to approach the problem, but there may be approaches that are less effective than others.

In these types of situations, a creative, never-give-up, problem-solving mentality is required. The best strategy and operations consultants have this capacity.

Takeaway Exercise: Try to find the most difficult project within your company or firm. At minimum, learn about the problem. If possible learn about how people are addressing that problem and whether you might be able to help.

28
EMPATHY VERSUS SYMPATHY IN CONSULTING

I've had some interesting discussions on how corporate politics play a role when consulting with clients. Perhaps I have a parochial view. My take is that consultants should take no part in corporate politics.

Here's a rationale for no politics. Consultants are often brought in to make things better. Clients pay a premium for consultants for any number of reasons. One common reason is that consultants are supposed to be unbiased third parties. If one gets consumed in politics, there's not enough focus on the end goal.

Here's another way to look at things. In consulting, empathy is the ability to understand what a person is going through. Sympathy goes one step further. One not only understands a person, but also agrees with the person on an emotional level.

But sympathy can be bad for consultants. Suppose one is working with a business unit sponsored by one of the executives, and there are two VPs organizationally below the executive that don't get along with one another. You are alone in the office with one of the VPs that you may like better from a personal chemistry point of view, and this VP starts to bad mouth the other VP. If you join into this sort of thing, while you may be ingratiating yourself with the one VP, you are hurting the client by participating in politics. Bad mouthing is just not constructive. In this sort of scenario, you should probably consider something like letting the VP know that you can understand why they might feel this way, but that as a consultant, you can't have any part in this. Other good options might be to try to get the VPs to work it out face-to-face. One may also want to probe a bit with the VP to see if it is worthwhile to bring the situation to the attention of the sponsoring executive, especially if the dysfunctionality is hurting the productivity of the business.

So empathy skills are a definite must for consultants. Crossing the boundary between empathy and sympathy needs to be a very deliberate decision.

Takeaway Exercise: Finding the right way to express empathy in the moment is a lifelong skill. Explore some other perspectives from other consultants on empathy, such as by Charles Green in his post, "Trust Matters Blog: Why Saying 'I Understand' Is an Act of Arrogance" (Green 2009).

29
SECRET TECHNIQUES TO OVERCOMING OBSTACLES IN DYNAMIC SITUATIONS

Over the years, I have had to opportunity to manage different groups, and perhaps more importantly observe how different managers and consultants face obstacles. As with many other concepts in this book, often these techniques for addressing obstacles are passed down through mentorship or peer exchanges. As such, these techniques are less documented. Here are a few notable techniques that I've seen:

- **The Experiment** – In this case the obstacle that the manager wants to overcome is to make forward progress into an unknown area. For example, suppose a manager wants to adapt a software product for an adjacent customer market. The manager may allocate a budget to a small business development and delivery team to explore and develop a lead customer in the new market.
- **The Audition** – In some cases, the problem to be tackled is either new or the prime resource to deliver is an unknown. For example, suppose the manager needs someone to serve as the principal consultant to lead a new group of services professionals. The unspoken audition may be that the manager may want the principal to lead one engagement with key folks on the

delivery team as part of the engagement. The other aspect of the audition may be to have the candidate assist with proposal development and lead an aspect of a customer sales pitch meeting.

- **The Process Versus Milestones Approach** – Some situations arise where it is not possible for one group to dictate the larger process that a company (or another group) should follow. In these cases, the basis of the conversation can be shifted so that groups agree to measure key milestones and outputs. For example, suppose one internal group wants a sales organization to follow a certain process to control focus and quality of customer messaging. While the internal group may find it difficult to instill explicit processes within the other group, the two groups can agree to have review meeting milestones and measurements to assess focus and quality indirectly. So the technique is based on the concept that processes and milestones go hand-in-hand. If one has trouble on the process, try working from milestones angle instead.
- **The Associations Versus Strategic Approach** – Strategy ideally comes before tactics. However, strategy often requires a lot of top-down thinking and heavy analytical brainpower. For example, in top-down marketing one may need to define targeting and positioning methods after one has done a complete analysis of the customer segments, value propositions, competitors, company strengths, etc. Yet the battles in the field are happening today and right now. What are the soldiers supposed to do at this moment? Here's where intuitive thinking, improvisation, and emergent strategies come to mind. In these cases, immediate tactics are based on doing something consistent with what has been done in the past, creating connections, or taking actions that create consistent associations (such as consistent brand associations whether the brand association strategy itself is valid).

There are obviously many more techniques that managers use for overcoming obstacles in dynamic situations, but I like these in particular because they address uncertainty and risk associated with different business aspects, such as projects, people, process, or strategy.

Takeaway Exercise: If you haven't spent time learning about improv, try exploring. Two papers that would be good to consider reading include "Stand Up and Throw Away the Script" (Susan 2003) and "Leadership Agility: Using Improv to Build Critical Skills" (Kelly 2012).

30
HOW TO SMOOTH TRANSITIONS AT PROJECT COMPLETION

Eventually projects between clients and consultants come to an end. Similar to completion of a good run as an employee of a firm, feelings at the end of a consulting project can be bittersweet. For me, the sweetness of successfully completing a project feels great; while the end of the day-to-day, close working relationship with the client can make one feel sentimental.

Over the years I've learned of some tricks:

- **Clients and consultants should develop a mutual understanding of how the relationship will eventually end in terms of time of transition.** While we don't need pre-nuptials, recognize that relationship communication is a two-way street. Some consulting partners explicitly discuss with client executives the notion of gradually winding down longer-term relationships over periods of months (versus days or weeks) so that business and operational needs are met.
- **The mutual understanding of project duration with clients and consultants may be specified in terms of project phases.** Using product development lifecycle terms, the two parties may define a relationship scope to be around early phases such as

ideation, planning, design, development, and incubation versus ongoing management. A twist on this may be identifying the strategic roadmap, blue sky, whiteboard areas, etc. that the client will work on regardless of consultant involvement and then picking where the consultant will work. Once the areas are complete, the client-consultant relationship will end.

- **Support the transition process with documentation, project closeout meetings, and the like.** These are basic project management fundamentals, and in the cases where project boundaries may be less clear (e.g., due to a long-term relationship with a client), having tangible outputs and milestone events can help parties to transition.
- **In cases of certain strategic initiative, interim management, and special-situation consulting arrangements, transition success can be measured by how effective permanent hires are onboarded.** The tactical transitions can include the consultant helping with securing new financial budgets for an organization, providing knowledge transfer of strategy and planning efforts, shadowing new hires, and helping to build out ongoing operational processes.

Takeaway Exercise: To prepare for the end of a project, it can be helpful to think about two outcomes on different ends of the spectrum or ask your reports to go through this exercise. First imagine the project ended amazingly. Describe the outcome and the steps leading up to that amazing ending, such as in terms of scope, people, communication, preparation, process. Next imagine the project ended very poorly. Describe the outcome and the steps leading up to the woeful ending. Now think about whether there are additional things you might do for your current project to help improve the odds of success.

SECTION FOUR: CONSULTING SPECIAL SITUATIONS

31
ON CONDUCTING COMPETITIVE INTELLIGENCE ETHICALLY

Competitive intelligence (CI) is an activity done by a wide range of professionals ranging from marketers to product managers to consultants to strategic planners. For many years I held back on writing about the subject of conducting CI ethically. I tend to be more on the conservative side, and by writing down my thoughts on this subject publicly, I had concerns that some clients and future employers would see me as too soft on the issue. Would a client shy away from hiring me because I was unwilling to go the distance to get a job done?

In spite of my concerns, I've decided to address the issue here. In my experience with the business world, I've seen the topic of ethics, in the context of CI, discussed much less frequently than I would have expected, and that should change. I'll provide some examples of bread and butter methods and more infrequently used methods for conducting CI. I'll also provide some examples of activities that I either think are questionable or outright unethical.

Here are some examples of ethical, secondary research methods for performing CI:

- Pulling annual reports and shareholder presentations on competitors from the web.

- Analyzing Securities and Exchange Commission (SEC) filings and financial statements.
- Gathering marketing collateral information from trade show booths of competitors.
- Obtaining industry reports from investment banks and/or financial institutions.
- Reverse engineering the positioning focus of competitors from marketing collateral.
- Searching through LinkedIn to analyze sales force profiles and reverse engineer likely go-to-market methods.
- Analyzing resumes of employees of competitor.
- Using Google satellite to analyze geographic profile and size of competitor facilities.
- Using CrunchBase or TechCrunch to analyze private companies.
- Using Compete, Alexa, and other web services to analyze web traffic.
- Analyzing advertising copy and positioning.
- Purchasing third-party reports (e.g., Gartner, Forrester, Parks Associates) to round out research.
- Looking through job postings by the company on the web.

Here are some examples of ethical, primary research methods for performing CI:

- Interviewing a distributor that has experience with competitors and asking questions whether client's proposed offer would be competitive.
- Asking distributor to describe any non-confidential information that they would be comfortable sharing about either the competitor or distributor's relationship with competitor.
- Visiting retail outlets of competitor to infer go-to-market methods, assess general profile of locations, etc.
- Directly purchasing a competitor's service or product.
- Surveying salespeople within client organization to get their feedback on what they've run into with respect to

selling against the competition.

- Conducting focus groups with general customers to get their feedback on competitor's products versus the client's prospective offerings.
- Obtaining general information by calling into a competitor's call center.

Finally, here are some examples of questionable or unethical methods of performing CI. These topics come up somewhat frequently in my experience:

- Misrepresenting oneself as a potential customer of competitor in order to get pricing information not made generally public.
- Asking a current distributor or employee of competitor to share proprietary information about competitors and violate non-disclosure agreements.
- Interviewing a competitor's employees for the sole purpose of gathering competitive information as opposed to intending to consider such people for direct hire.

One problem that I see organizations run into is that they can get focused on one single issue. For example, they may say, "I must know exactly how competitor X is pricing their product." This type of logic can be dangerous because it tends to lead to one solution. It may also tempt one to try to take unethical shortcuts. If the problem statement is reframed around "getting a better picture of whether my client's market offer is competitive," then this can lead to more flexible types of solutions. Tools like conducting customer focus groups, surveying salespeople, etc. then become possibilities for solving the real problem at hand.

As a closing note, one way to think about activities is to classify them in two dimensions: ethical/unethical and legal/illegal. Another framework that I use for weighing ethical issues is to determine how I would feel if my activities were plastered all over major press outlets. Would my team or personal activities embarrass me? Posing that type of question is often a nice litmus test for good behavior.

Takeaway Exercise: Explore other specialized sources on competitive intelligence practices. For example, review

the code of ethics as outlined on the website for Strategic and Competitive Intelligence Professionals (SCIP Code of Ethics for CI Professionals n.d.).

32
SWEARING BY OR SWEARING AT BENCHMARKING

Some consultants swear by benchmarking. Benchmarking client company operations against comparable company operations helps to place the client company in the context of competition, quantify areas of differences, and provide a fact-based foundation upon which management decisions can be made. Yet during execution one can run into a ton of issues, some of which include:

- Benchmark information cannot be readily found.
- Existing benchmarks are collected for a service or product, which is not comparable to the service or product of current concern.
- Validity of some of the benchmarks is questionable and more broadly undermine the credibility of your case.
- Client metrics don't exist, are questionable, or turn out to be less comparable after having expended effort to collect.

Given the issues above, it's not unusual to find oneself swearing at benchmarking. And we've not even mentioned the perspective that benchmarking against terrible companies is often fundamentally flawed.

In the spirit of looking for alternatives or complements to

benchmarking operations, consider some other approaches:

- **Structural Analysis** – For example, whether operations processes can be run in parallel versus serial is something that can be factually analyzed and need not necessarily be compared to other companies.
- **Bottleneck Analysis** – For example, when resources are waiting downstream for another resource that is bottlenecked and when this situation happens frequently, this can indicate that the work structure is not optimal. Perhaps flattening of the work structure, cross-training, or better planning is desirable.
- **Trend Analysis** – For example, if costs are going up, cycle-times to respond are getting longer, and customers are getting more upset, these are facts that one can respond to without having to have extensive benchmarking data up-front. Note that while some companies do an okay job getting static data, many can improve their ability to get time-series data.
- **Goals and Consistency Analysis** – For example, if a company chooses a particular strategy (e.g., being a feature leader versus low-cost provider), then there are some tactics that are more or less consistent with the strategy (e.g., being a feature leader and running below average R&D investment rates reflects a potential inconsistency between strategy and tactics).

So before you start on a path toward benchmarking, make sure to step back and look at the bigger picture.

Takeaway Exercise: Read the article "When Benchmarks Don't Work" (Kaplan 2006).

33
A PEEK AT THE DIFFICULTIES OF INCUBATING NEW INITIATIVES WITHIN LARGE COMPANIES

Entrepreneurial situations in large companies differ from those of startups, yet one thing that they seem to share is that they often represent hope in one way or another. In the case of large corporations, these new initiatives can not only turn out to be profitable ventures, but also boost morale and reward key employees through growth opportunities. Yet many of these new initiatives have difficulty getting off the ground. Frustration is common. This section provides a peek at some of the situations, complexities, and steps to resolution that I have seen.

First, here's a picture of a common situation in a large company faced with the prospect of starting a new initiative or business line:

- Perceivably significant, yet amorphous, business opportunity.
- No money committed and no budget.
- Limited organizational resources.
- Established products and sales & marketing channels.
- Mature, complex business and product approval processes.

What adds a level of complexity to the situation, and sometimes leads to insanity for those working directly within the environment, is that:

- Ventures require substantial investment to ultimately succeed.
- Finance cycle of start-up opportunities (opportunity timing) does not align well with the long, finance planning cycles of large companies.
- Star players in the current organization have limited availability for the new organization.
- Articulating and aligning on a business opportunity requires collaboration by many functions, and these functions are separate and overloaded in the current organization.
- Sales and product development processes often need to be understood at more than the surface-level.

Here are some ideas for addressing many of the above issues:

- Recognize that it's not usually possible or desirable to speed up the process by cutting corners.
- Break the process into smaller pieces to get rolling.
- Search for the right sponsor and core team.
- Secure a portion of time for each of the star players.
- Give the employees a real chance to make things work.
- Consider getting a commitment for small amount of money to get rolling.
- Start to articulate what the business opportunity looks like and document it.
- Consider using a facilitator that can pull the pieces together, help layout program plan, and frame strategic issues and options.
- Paint the vision for the organizational structure and build emotional attachment to the cause.
- Involve those from sales and product development that will be eager to provide input and testing grounds.
- Aim for pioneer sales and business development deals with lighthouse accounts. Concrete wins.

- Rinse, refine, increase commitment, and repeat.

It may take a leap of faith to get things started. Sometimes the keys are to look for forward motion and to take some initial steps as opposed to wanting to knock it out of the park too soon.

Takeaway Exercise: Spend fifteen minutes investigating an existing, entrepreneurial activity in your industry with a large organization (perhaps your own). Learn about what worked and didn't work.

34
CONTRASTING WINNING AND LOSING STARTUP MOVES WITHIN LARGER COMPANIES

Companies looking to incubate new businesses or start-up climates within a larger company are challenging situations to get off the ground. Based on consulting to and working with companies in these types of situations, here are some thoughts on winning and losing moves:

Sponsorship and Structure

Having a start-up sponsor in name or position only is generally a losing move. Successful, external startups have managers that will fight to win, pave new ground, work out kinks, get the best resources, etc. If the sponsor is a senior executive that provides only oversight, does not push or provide guidance, and does not empower delegates, this could be a warning sign for an effort that will not bear fruit. If you have a start-up sponsor that provides political and boundary management only, then it might be a good idea to get a powerful delegate that answers to the sponsor and can help to "fly cover" in the organization. Situations where cover may be needed include designing new marketing material, getting special access to the sales team, breaking new ground in the legal contracts area, and getting financial budgets approved outside of normal, overly conservative control mechanisms.

Strategy and Goals

Failing to clearly articulate the ultimate goal and problem statement of the startup early on is another losing move. On the other end of the spectrum, making the strategy too complicated is probably another losing move. For example, when faced with the startup options of creating new revenue, helping cross-sell other services within the larger company, reducing customer churn, etc., I would generally lean away from trying to knock down too many at once. All options can be on the radar and should be part of early brainstorming and strategy sessions. That said, viewing the startup as a standalone, instead of totally integrated, unit may be the best option of getting traction first.

Core Team and Extended Resources

Many organizations fail to bring in new blood when new blood is needed. At risk of disrespecting both large company- and entrepreneur-types, these two often don't understand one another. For example, entrepreneur-types may lack respect for large company processes. This can be dangerous though, because buy-in and tapping into the resources (e.g., financing, intellectual property, extended team resources, channels) of a large company can be tremendous. On the other hand, large company employees can become accustomed to the culture, pace, and processes of the existing business. These may be incompatible with aspects of a new venture. Bringing in new blood for a start-up within a larger company is often a winning move, and resources need to be different and complementary.

In closing, while getting the right cadence (e.g., activities, milestones, timing) for the startup opportunity is important, so is establishing the right environment and tone.

Takeaway Exercise: If you did the exercise in the previous chapter, now think about what worked and didn't work with a closer focus on sponsorship and

structure, strategy and goals, and core team and extended resources.

35
THE BUSINESS PLAN IS ALIVE AND WELL BUT IT MAY NOT BE WHAT YOU THINK

As many times I have written a business plan as a consultant or manager, the flavor can vary substantially. Why? While many textbook approaches and templates have similar structures, the perspective that gets lost in the mix is intent. The intent of a business plan affects its format and content dramatically. Here I thought it would be good to share some perspectives as to when and where things should vary.

Business plan as a process - The process of vetting ideas, getting buy-in, and achieving alignment is most important in these situations. Example situations are new business launches in larger companies. Business plans can often take the form of workshop sessions and PowerPoint, as opposed to a traditional Word documents. For a complementary perspective, see Chapter 11: In Consulting the Process is an Essential Part of the Deliverable.

Business plan as a sales document - This situation is particularly appropriate for fund raising. Key goals of the document are to establish trust with prospects, enable the investment idea to be shared with network connections, and persuade people of the merits of an investment opportunity. One often needs a mix of instruments (e.g., PowerPoint and

Word documents, napkin drawings, demo) depending on the team, industry, and lifecycle phase of product development.

Business plan as an investigative framework – An entrepreneurial way of looking at a business plan is more as a set of hypotheses and questions. Example questions may include to what extent do customers really want product A, do customers prefer one variation over another, and do customers perceive our offering as Y relative to competitors? The business planning effort can be more organic and involve focus groups, customer prospect interviews, etc. But the overall process should be systematic in determining which hypotheses are true or false to prove out aspects the business. Readers may be interested in methods consistent with lean approaches, such as the Business Model Canvas at www.businessmodelgeneration.com and Lean Canvas at www.leanstack.com.

There are surely other ways to look at a business plan, such as a stage gate requirement for product development or due diligence exhibit for government grants. The real key is to take a step back and really think about the goals of the effort.

Takeaway Exercise: The next time you develop a business plan, think about the perspectives above. To what extent do one or more of these fit your situation?

36
WHAT TO DO WHEN YOUR PROFESSIONAL SERVICES ORGANIZATION IS NOT PROFESSIONAL ENOUGH

In this book, I wanted to address professional services organizations as they are closely related to consulting organizations. While on one end of the spectrum some people and organizations take a strict perspective that professional services are limited to services that tie directly to a product, there are others that are broader and provide traditional consulting services within their professional services organization.

With that as backdrop, some companies have asked me to develop, tune-up, or reboot their professional services organizations. During the discovery and assessment phase, here are some things that I've heard:

- Customer: "Instead of providing consulting services, your organization is marketing its products to me and asking me to pay the bill."
- General manager of services organization: "I am not sure we know what services we sell versus what services are provided as part of the product pre-sales cycle."

- Manager of services organization: "We have a project in X area, we're doing another thing with company Y, and we also have a lot of internal work on Z. It's really hard to report on where our time is spent."
- Customer: "The consultants you've assigned seem to have good technical and analytical skills. I am not sure what they are doing to help me, though."
- Field manager: "Customer A is pretty much dead and will need a restart. We got to step 10 in the process before we realized our services team forgot to perform step 2 for quality control."
- Manager of services: "How do we price jobs? How do we cost jobs? No particular method."
- General services manager: "Our folks have traditionally provided services for free, and now we are trying to charge money for them because the services have value. But our quality is not there, and we don't have the discipline built into our DNA."

One way to think about fixing these organizations is from the ground-up:

- **Inventory the delivery team** - What skills do these folks have on the technical side? What soft skills do they have in terms of dealing with clients? How can we develop the team's leadership skills?
- **Inspect either the project management or engagement management areas** - To what extent is a cadence and communication structure established between the organization and the customer? Have there been frameworks or tools developed to support the customer-facing processes? Are there knowledge management processes in place to help with delivering greater value to the customer? What role does mentorship and apprenticeship play in the organization?
- **Analyze the sales process and key contacts with customer organization** - What is the strategy for services? Do we have a crisp story on getting from needs to solutions and services? Do we proactively manage the sales pipeline? Who owns and follows-

through on key customer contact points? Is there a customer satisfaction process that involves both direct parties delivering and independent parties objectively evaluating the quality of services delivered?

- **Assess what's next for customers and how your company's boundaries fit into a larger, whole solution for the customer** - What role should thought leadership play? How can the services organization figure out how greater value can be added to the customer experience? Should we expand the offerings? Should we partner with other companies? Or maybe we should change the total mix of products and services so that the customer can derive additional value on their own?

Professional services organizations are complex, and the above framework enables one to start to think about how one can make improvements that affect services delivered today, while keeping other areas in perspective for handling down the road.

Takeaway Exercise: The next time you encounter a professional sales organization, do a quick inventory and rate them on the four dimensions of quality of individuals, engagement management skill, sales and relationship management, whole solution fit.

37
STARTING CONSULTING SERVICES ORGANIZATIONS WITHIN PRODUCT COMPANIES

When people think about consultants, they often think about those that work for companies like Accenture, Bain, Deloitte, McKinsey, PwC, etc. These are companies that are traditionally independent from product vendors. However, there are a number of companies that provide consulting or professional services as part of product companies (e.g., companies like Cisco, Ericsson, IBM, Oracle) that may sell things like hardware or software. I've had the opportunity to incubate or reboot the management, sales, marketing, and delivery for a number of these types of services organizations, and they definitely face a number of issues that are unique from independent consulting firms.

Based on my experience with looking at these type types of organizations from an end-to-end view, here are four common failure points:

- **Unclear strategy for providing consulting services** – An example of unclear strategy includes not being able to articulate to what extent consulting services should be designed to protect product lines, versus providing a new revenue stream. Also, the organization should be able to articulate the services portfolio, which consists of the types of consulting services to be provided.

- **Unclear method for getting leads into the pipeline** – Depending on strategy, consulting services organizations within product companies are often implemented as overlay organizations, and as such, the process of getting in front of customers and managing prospects can lack proper definition, discipline, and support tools. Often the buyer in the organization is different too.
- **Improper tones for sales meetings** – Product companies are often used to marketing-push type sales strategies. On the other hand, consulting services sales are often more diagnosis, empathy, and problem solving oriented. Getting the right mix between product and services messaging takes some work.
- **Irregular quality of consulting services project delivery** – In some cases, consulting services may be may be provided as an afterthought or on a "free" basis to customers; subsidized by product sales. Unfortunately, a customer's time is money, so even if the service cost is covered elsewhere, the consulting organization still needs to provide quality work to the customer.

Note that the figure below is something that I've adapted for this special situation based on original, more general work by Ford Harding (Harding 1998).

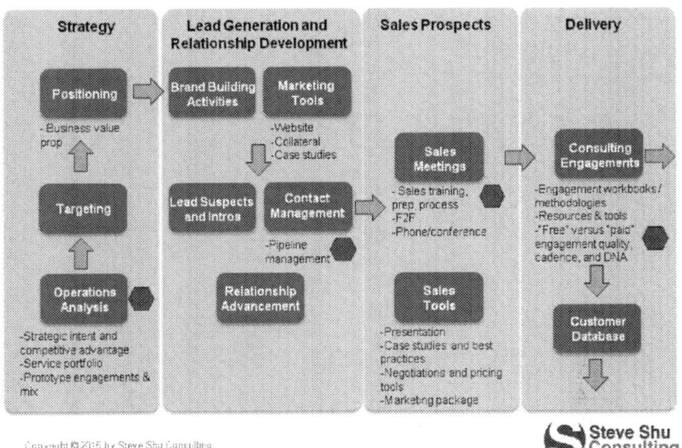

Downloadable figure available at: http://steveshuconsulting.com/2000/01/download-figures-the-consulting-apprenticeship

Implementing consulting organizations within product companies can be a great opportunity. That said, there are hazards involved with getting these organizations seated properly and kept on track. Having a framework like the one above to discuss and address these issues can be very helpful.

Takeaway Exercise: If you are interested in services as related to product companies, consider reading the paper "The Right Services Strategy for Product Companies" (Auguste, Harmon and Pandit 2006).

38
INTEGRATING BEHAVIORAL ECONOMICS AND CONSULTING

Since I have been involved with a number of projects that utilize behavioral economics principles to improve outcomes or change people's behavior, I thought I would share some thoughts on integrating behavioral economics into the practice of consulting.

For those unfamiliar with the term "behavioral economics," I generally describe behavioral economics as a combination of psychology and a traditional science like economics or finance. Whereas models in traditional economics and finance often assume that people are supercomputers and maximize their utility over numerous dimensions, behavioral economics tries to be more descriptive of actual behavior and account for the beauty and shortcomings of the human mind and spirit. For example, why do some people help or punish others when it is not in their best economics interests to do so? Why do some people not help themselves (e.g., fail to save enough for retirement) when they clearly can from other measures and/or field testing? How do we know when a commercial or public system has been set up in a behaviorally unfriendly way, and what can or should be done about it?

These last questions get at the heart of one model I have seen for integrating behavioral economics into the consulting model. This model is the notion of integrating behavioral audits and recommendations into the consulting process.

For example in *Save More Tomorrow* (Benartzi 2012)[3], Dr. Shlomo Benartzi introduced the notion of a behavioral audit for 401(k) and defined contribution plans. In such an audit, questions are asked to the effect of:

- Do employees have to opt-in or opt-out relative to joining the 401(k) plan? (This question addresses the behavioral challenge of inertia.)
- Are employee savings rates automatically escalated when a person gets a pay raise? (This question addresses the behavioral challenge of loss aversion.)
- Do participants get 401(k) statements that show projected income at retirement? (This question addresses the behavioral challenge of myopia.)

The behavioral audit then opens the door for strategic recommendations, such as defaulting employees into plan or at least providing them easy ways to get into a plan, changing employer match rates, restructuring choices in the investment menu, etc. If a company wants to go really deep on implementation, they have an opportunity to work with their consultant or financial advisor to create options, prioritize, and work on an implementation plan.

More generally, the notion of a behavioral audits and recommendations can be designed to assess many other processes. For example, how well does a software application work from a behavioral perspective in terms of getting people to take action? How effective are our management dashboards and processes for managing a portfolio of projects? How good is our website in terms of disseminating information and facilitating choices?

Beyond audits and strategic recommendations, there's also a tremendous opportunity to apply behavioral economics principles to a second area: the design and implementation phases of consulting projects. Behavioral economics recognizes

---

[3] Disclosure: I helped with development of behavioral finance books, supporting programs, tools, and software product management while working as a consultant to Allianz Global Investors Center for Behavioral Finance.

that people are influenced by things that won't make a difference to a robot, but do matter to humans. We have to pay a lot more attention to design, because design is there whether intended or not. And any design architecture, explicitly or implicitly, imposes a value system. Such a value system could be to maximize value for a specific party. Another value system might be to do the most good for the most people.

So where to start?

A first step is to open your eyes more broadly to behavioral economics. I think that cross-functional disciplines, whether behavioral economics or other, tend to be underappreciated because appreciation requires knowledge that cut across areas that are not traditionally combined.

A second step is developing a good base of knowledge regarding behavioral economics and applications. You can do this by working with people experienced in the area. You can also start to get introduced to these concepts through reading books like *Nudge* (Thaler and Sunstein 2009) or *Thinking, Fast and Slow* (Kahneman 2013). Although I am biased since I was part of team to help with the book, Benartzi's *Save More Tomorrow* is a great book for shedding light on how behavioral economics principles are applied in detail to a very specific problem: design of defined contribution plans for retirement savings.

A third step is recognizing that while it is important to draw from research and core principles done by academics and from certain areas of the industry, it is important to test your application of behavioral economics, whether that application be for consulting, a solution, or a product. Sometimes we think one behavioral principle will apply in a scenario when something else turns out to be the case. The use of solid behavioral principles based on research help guide, and should improve the odds of success.

Takeaway Exercise: If you are just learning about behavioral economics, read the article about Daniel Kahneman by Michael Lewis, "The Kind of Human Error" (Lewis 2011).

39
WHETHER TO PROVIDE FEEDBACK ON CLIENT STAFF TO CLIENT MANAGEMENT AS A CONSULTANT

It is a tricky question that comes up in some consulting situations. Suppose you are helping with an assessment of a client company's operations. You are working throughout the organization with line managers and other personnel. The client sponsor asks you for professional feedback about full-time employees within the client organization. How honest should you be with your feedback? What should you do or what should you advise others to do within the engagement team?

My general rule of thumb on this topic is to:

- Tread very carefully.
- Try to avoid commenting on staff.
- If you must comment, be clinical and precise on the context and the limitations of your observation or interaction with staff. Make sure you think through both positives and negatives of client staff performance.

Here are some reasons for my thinking:

- A consultant is usually an outsider and does not have to live with the implications of giving positive or negative feedback.

- Observation periods are often short, since limited to a subset of the engagement period, which may be days or weeks.
- Consultants are often hired to address a particular problem statement for the client, and unless the charter was to evaluate employees, which in most cases it is not except for niche practices or statements of work, then your perspectives may not be grounded enough.
- Consulting engagements often require working up and down the chain of organizational structure, and your reputation and effectiveness as a consultant could be damaged if people think that you are talking about them or evaluating them behind their backs.
- You must be extra careful that you have not been unduly biased prior to the evaluation request by either the client sponsor or other significant players in the client organization.

That said, an understandable fear may be that the client sponsor will not look to you as a trusted adviser if you do not provide your perspectives. Many consultants would argue that the client is paying you good money and that you need to provide your perspectives. The ground can be tough here. Be clinical, think through pros and cons, and couch your caveats. Above all, act responsibly and ethically.

Takeaway Exercise: If you are a consultant practitioner, exchange ideas about how to approach these situations with a peer or mentor.

40
CONSULTING VERSUS INTERIM MANAGEMENT

Whether to use consultants versus interim managers can be a bit of a loaded topic, and I won't attempt to address every angle here. Rather, I want to share some color based on anecdotal experiences.

To set the context, here's a couple of working definitions that I'll offer up:

- **Consulting** – Use of a third-party (potentially a team) to help a company solve a particular business problem. For example, evaluate business opportunity for offering mobility applications to consumers; provide an independent assessment of a call center that is performing questionably.
- **Interim Management** – For a limited period of time or trial period, use of one or more experienced individuals to take or play the role of a manager or executive within the company.

I first started to pay attention to the term "interim management" when I worked back in the 1990s at the management consulting firm Pittiglio Rabin Todd and McGrath (PRTM, acquired by PwC). PRTM was a firm that balanced strategy and operations engagements. As such, the firm got involved with both early strategic planning and later-phase, tactical design of business capabilities. At risk of oversimplifying, PRTM consultants were not just pure strategy people, but they were often people with actual implementation and management experience. There was a firm motto that floated around, "Results, Not Reports." This motto was essentially a shot at strategy firm practices of delivering stacks of analyses and reports that never had an impact. I remember one of the partners, who had just rolled off an assignment as interim CEO, describing to me his view on interim management. He said something to the effect of: "Interim management is something [infrequent] that the firm only does for special clients. Unless approached correctly, interim management can create a dependency between the firm consultant and the client that is hard to wean the parties off of. But interim management can offer a variety of benefits, particularly when a company wants to move forward with operational execution immediately."

Since then, here are a few examples I've heard from clients over the years, which are indicative of a lean more towards use of interim management over consulting approaches:

- "We don't have the management skill set internally, and we need to fill three management roles in finance, services, and technology pretty immediately while introducing more sophisticated practices that can be transferred to the larger organization as we grow."
- "We are exploring this new geography for our products and services, and we need someone to help us as a general executive (covering all entity and operational requirements) to see if we can get things to pan out."
- "Our marketing VP will be going out on parental leave, and we need someone to fill the role for six- to nine-months."
- "We need someone that can fulfill the corporate development function with total dedication, but we need the option to release this person once we have met the objective of securing a beachhead in the North America enterprise market."

While there are clearly tradeoffs to using interim managers or transitioning consultants to interim managers, my personal experience is that these setups can work quite well provided that timing is right and that you find the right resource and weigh the potential risks.

Takeaway Exercise: Seek out opportunities to meet people who have worked in interim management roles. Learn about the scope of their roles and potential contracting differences from consulting relationships. You may also want to investigate the websites of professional associations within the UK, as the UK tends to be more advanced than other countries in terms of the use of interims.

SUMMARY

Thank you for reading. If you've gotten this far, you definitely deserve a medal. I hope that you took away some new perspectives from the book and perhaps learned something new. I wrote this book because I am passionate about the professional practice of consulting. I aspire to the principles I shared in Chapter 22: Management Consulting Manifesto. If you haven't already done so, I hope that you develop your own manifesto.

As I mentioned in the introduction, mastery is a lifelong journey. I'm sure I'll find new things to share. When I document other thoughts and resources, I will make them available at www.consultingapprenticeship.com.

In the meantime, good luck. Please feel free to reach me at steve@steveshuconsulting.com and let me know your thoughts.

Best wishes and warmest regards,

Stephen Shu

BIBLIOGRAPHY

Auguste, Byron, Eric Harmon, and Vivek Pandit. "The right services strategy for product companies." *The McKinsey Quarterly*, 2006: 41-51.

Benartzi, Shlomo. *Save More Tomorrow: Practical Behavioral Finance Solutions to Improve 401(k) Plans*. 2012.

Block, Peter. *Flawless Consulting: A Guide to Getting Your Expertise Used.* Pfeiffer, 2011.

Green, Charles. *Trust Matters Blog: Why Saying 'I Understand' Is an Act of Arrogance.* September 22, 2009. http://trustedadvisor.com/trustmatters/Why-Saying-I-Understand-Is-an-Act-of-Arrogance (accessed April 28, 2015).

Harding, Ford. *Creating Rainmakers: The Manager's Guide to Training Professionals to Attract Clients.* Adams Media Corporation, 1998.

Harding, Ford. *Rain Making: Attract New Clients No Matter What Your Field.* Adams Media Corporation, 2008.

Kahneman, Daniel. *Thinking, Fast and Slow.* Farrar, Straus and Gioroux, 2013.

Kaplan, Robert. "When Benchmarks Don't Work." *Harvard Business School Working Knowledge.* January 9, 2006. http://hbswk.hbs.edu/item/5158.html (accessed April 28, 2015).

Kelly, Kip. "Leadership Agility: Using Improv to Build Critical Skills." *Kenan-Flagler Business School.* 2012. http://execdev.kenan-flagler.unc.edu/leadership-agility-using-improv (accessed April 28, 2015).

Kouzes, James, and Barry Posner. *The Leadership Challenge: How to Make Extraordinary Things Happen in Organizations.* Jossey-Bass, 2012.

Lewis, Michael. "The King of Human Error." Vanity Fair News. December 2011. http://www.vanityfair.com/news/2011/12/michael-lewis-201112 (accessed April 29, 2015).

Maister, David H. *Managing the Professional Service Firm.* Free Press, 1997.

McKee, Robert. *Story: Substance, Structure, Style and the Principles of Screenwriting.* ReganBooks, 1997.

McLaughlin, Michael W. *Winning the Professional Services Sale.* Wiley, 2009.

Merriam-Webster, Incorporated. "Previous Wrods of the Year." *Merriam-Webster.* http://www.merriam-webster.com/info/07words_prev.htm (accessed March 12, 2015).

Minto, Barbara. *The Pyramid Principle: Logic in Writing and Thinking.* Prentice Hall, 2010.

PwC Completes Acquisition of PRTM. August 22, 2011. http://www.prnewswire.com/news-releases/pwc-completes-acquisition-of-prtm-128201798.html (accessed March 3, 2015).

Rasiel, Ethan M. *The McKinsey Way: Using the Techniques of the World's Top Strategic Consultants to Help You and Your Business.* McGraw-Hill, 1999.

Schein, Edgar H. *Process Consultation.* FT Press, 1988.

SCIP Code of Ethics for CI Professionals. https://www.scip.org/CodeOfEthics.php (accessed April 28, 2015).

Senge, Peter. *The Fifth Discipline: The Art & Practice of The Learning Organization.* Doubleday, 2006.

Susan, Parker. "Stand Up and Throw Away the Script." *Harvard Management Communication Letter*, 2003: 3-5.

Thaler, Richard, and Cass Sunstein. *Nudge: Improving Decisions About Health, Wealth, and Happiness.* Penguin Books, 2009.

Time, Inc. "Person of the Year: You." *Time Magazine.* December 25, 2006. http://content.time.com/time/covers/0,16641,20061225,00.ht

ml (accessed March 12, 2015).

Verganti, Roberto. *Design Driven Innovation: Changing the Rules of Competition by Radically Innovating What Things Mean.* Harvard Business Press, 2009.

ABOUT THE AUTHOR

Steve Shu provides management consulting and business development services. He specializes in incubating new initiatives and business lines with primary focus on services and technology. Steve has held a number consulting and management roles at Allianz Global Investors Center for Behavioral Finance, Allscripts, Nortel Business Consulting, Pittiglio Rabin Todd and McGrath (acquired by PwC), and numerous startups. Steve has also been an Assistant Professor in the business school at Irvine University and an Account Director for the Taproot Foundation.

Steve holds an MBA from the University of Chicago and both an ME and BS in Electrical Engineering from Cornell University.

Steve can be reached using the contact information available at steveshuconsulting.com

Made in the USA
Middletown, DE
05 February 2017